POKER

Is the Name of the Game

Walter Gibson

Harper & Row, Publishers
New York, Hagerstown, San Francisco, London

POKER
CONTENTS

NOTE

In the pages that follow, as common Poker terms are introduced and described, they will be given *in italics,* so the reader can familiarize himself with them in proceeding through the book.

I

MODERN POKER

Originally known as Bluff, modern Poker has many forms, all based on the early game, so its description will help clarify the rest. Five cards are dealt to each player and starting at the dealer's left, each can either *pass* or *open* the betting by placing chips in the center pot.

From then on, each player may *call,* by meeting the amount already bet; or he may *raise,* by adding extra chips; or he may *drop* from the betting entirely, throwing his hand face down. When all bets have been called, there is a *showdown* in which the hands are compared and the one with the highest combination according to an accepted schedule, is the winner of the pot.

The element of bluff occurs when a player raises a bet on a weak hand, forcing out players with stronger hands who think he has them beaten. So the higher the stakes, the greater the opportunity for bluffing as opponents may *drop* rather than *stay* unless they have very strong hands.

Standard Hands

Hands are valued according to the following combinations which are accompanied by the approximate chances of being dealt such hands. A 52 card pack is used, running A, K, Q, J,

10, 9, 8, 7, 6, 5, 4, 3, 2; the Ace is sometimes rated low as well as high. Suits figure in special hands — as described — but no suit takes precedence over another.

ROYAL FLUSH   ♠: A,K,Q,J,10
The top five cards in any one suit. Chance: 1 out of 650,000.

STRAIGHT FLUSH   ♦: J,10,9,8,7
Five cards of the same suit in sequence. If two players hold such hands, the one with the highest card wins. The lowest possible Straight Flush is a Five High — ♣: 5,4,3,2,A — with the Ace counting as low card. Chance: 1 out of 65,000.

FOUR OF A KIND   A♠,A♣,A♦,A♥,9♠
Four Aces, the highest possible set of four, wins over any other fours. The odd card has no significance. Chance: 1 out of 4,000.

FULL HOUSE   J♦,J♠,J♥,4♣,4♦
Three cards of one value, two of another. Hand with the highest three wins over any other Full. Chance: 1 out of 700.

FLUSH   K♠,9♠,8♠,5♠,3♠
                                                      J♦,10♦,7♦,5♦,2♦
                                                      J♣,10♣,6♣,4♣,3♣
Five cards of the same suit, but not in numerical order. Flush with the highest card wins. If two have high cards of the same value, the next card rates high and so on. Chance: 1 out of 500.

STRAIGHT   A♥,K♣,Q♦,J♣,10♠
                                                      9♠,8♣,7♣,6♦,5♠
                                                      5♣,4♦,3♠,2♣,A♦
Five cards in numerical order, but with mixed suits. An Ace high Straight is called a Broadway and beats all others, as a

8

Straight is determined by its high card, lowest possible Straight is a Five high with Ace counting low. Chance of any Straight: 1 out of 250.

THREE OF A KIND   9♥,9♠,9♣,K♣,4♦

As the name implies, three cards of the same numerical value, with two of different denominations. With two such hands, the one with the highest set of Triplets wins. Chance: 1 out of 50.

TWO PAIR   A♦,A♣,9♥,9♦,5♣
                                     J♠,J♦,8♣,8♦,7♠
                                     J♥,J♣,6♦,6♥,Q♣
                                     10♦,10♥,4♣,4♥,K♦
                                     10♠,10♣,4♦,4♠,Q♥

Two Pair of different denominations, with an extra card of another value. If two hands or more contain Two Pair, the one with the highest pair wins. If the top pairs are tied, the hand with the higher second pair wins. If the Two Pairs are identical, the player with the higher odd card wins. Chance: 1 out of 20.

PAIR   K♥,K♦,5♣,4♦,2♦
                                  J♥,J♦,Q♣,9♣,5♠
                                  J♠,J♥,Q♦,8♠,6♦

Two of a Kind in numerical value, with three of different denominations. If more than one hand has a Pair — as often happens — the highest Pair wins. If tied, highest odd card wins. Chances of a Pair: 1 out of 2⅓.

NO PAIR   A♦,K♦,Q♠,J♠,9♣
                                     Q♥,9♦,7♦,5♣,3♣
                                     7♥,5♠,4♦,3♦,2♠

A hand with no two cards of the same value, with more than one suit represented. Highest card denotes the winner of several such hands; if high cards are the same, second highest, and so on. The highest possible No Pair and the lowest possible are both shown here. Normally, an Ace cannot be rated as a low card in such hands.

Chances as stated refer to possibilities of receiving such hands in the deal of five cards, and are therefore important in calculating prospects of other players.

Other combinations are used in various types of poker as well as freak games. Such special hands follow.

Freak Hands

Besides the standard hands already listed, there are other combinations, some of which are widely accepted in certain areas of the country. They are all optional, so any group of players has the privilege of naming anything they want.

Big Bobtail: a four card Straight Flush, with any odd fifth card as — **Q♥, J♥, 10♥, 9♥, A♠**. Rates just below Four of a Kind.

Blaze: All picture cards as — **K♥, K♠, K♦, Q♣, J♠** or **Q♠, Q♦, J♣, J♥, K♣**. Rates just below a Full House. An actual Full House or Four of a Kind composed of all picture cards would be rated normally.

Big Dog: Ace high, Nine low of mixed suits, as — A, Q, J, 10, 9. Ranks just below a Flush.

Big Cat: King high, Eight low, of mixed suits, as — K, Q, J, 9, 8. Ranks just below a Big Dog.

Little Dog: Seven high, Deuce low of mixed suits, as — 7, 6, 5, 3, 2. Ranks just below a Big Cat.

Around the Corner Straight: A Straight with Four, Three, Deuce as high, continuing with King, Queen, Jack, below

Ace, as — 4, 3, 2, A, K; 3, 2, A, K, Q; 2, A, K, Q, J. These rate below other Straights.

Skip or Dutch Straight: Alternating cards of mixed suits in sequence as — K, J, 9, 7, 5 or 10, 8, 6, 4, 2. Just below a Straight.

Kilter: The lowest Skip, running 9, 7, 5, 3, A.

Pelter or Skeet: A hand of mixed suits with a Nine, a Five, a Deuce, and other cards separating them, as — 9, 8, 5, 4, 2 or 9, 7, 5, 3, 2. Just below a Kilter.

Little Bobtail: Three cards toward a Straight Flush as — **J ♦, 10 ♦, 9 ♦, K ♣, 5 ♠**. Just below Three of a Kind.

Four Flush: Four cards of one suit, with an odd, as — **8 ♦, 6 ♦, 3 ♦, 2 ♦, 9 ♠**. Valued just above a Pair in some games of Five Card Stud. In others, below a Pair, but better than an Ace high hand.

Four Straight: Four cards of mixed suits in sequence, as J, 10, 9, 8. May be valued just below a Four Flush.

II

DRAW POKER

For many years, Draw Poker has been regarded as the standard game, as it is simply an extension of the original form, utilizing an added feature called the *draw*.

The game is usually played by three to seven players. Each puts an *ante* in a *pot* in the center of the table. This ante consists of a specified number of chips.

Cards are dealt singly to each player, who may *pass* until someone *opens*. After that, players *drop*, *call*, or *raise*, as in the original game, until the totals are equal. If all players pass, the deal moves to the next man on the left, who puts up an additional ante.

If only one player stays, he automatically wins the pot, without even disclosing his hand. If two or more stay, they do not show their hands, until after each has made a *draw*. This consists of a player discarding any cards he does not want, and having others dealt to replace them.

Discards are made face down, and if the player is satisfied with his hand, he may *stand pat*, which means that he draws no cards at all. After the draw, betting is resumed. The player who opened can *bet* or *check the bet*, giving the betting privilege to the next active player to his left.

Once a bet is made, each succeeding player may call, raise or drop, as usual. After all bets have been checked or called, there is a showdown, and the player with the highest hand wins the pot.

The Draw

The draw is the great feature of Draw Poker and not only enables a player to improve his hand to the status of a winner, but may help him to bluff opponents, by giving them a false idea of his actual holdings. The usual procedures and prospects are as follows.

A Five Card Draw is made when a player has practically nothing in his hand. He simply wants a new hand, hoping to do better. But whatever he gets, he is stuck with, as there will be no further chance for improvement. Usually, such hands are thrown in and forgotten. With some groups, five card draws are not allowed.

A Four Card Draw is made on the strength of one high card, as an Ace or a King, which at least is a start to a better hand. But the chance of matching the high card for a Pair is about 1 out of 4, with the chance of anything better about the same as on the original deal. With some groups, four card draws are not allowable.

A Three Card Draw is usually made in hopes of improving a Pair, which the player retains while discarding three odd cards. The chance of such improvement is about 1 out of 3½.

As a desperation draw, a player may hold two unmatched cards, but even if they are high, as Ace and King, his chance of getting a high Pair is less than 1 in 2½, with little hope of anything higher.

A Two Card Draw is often made in hope of improving Three of a Kind which the player already holds. Chances of such improvement are a little better than 1 out of 10, and when an improvement is made chances are 2 out of 3 that it will be a Full House rather than Four of a Kind.

Many players will hold a Pair and an odd card, or *kicker*, while making a two card draw. Chances of improving the Pair are almost as good as with a three card draw, particularly if the *kicker* is an Ace or King, which may produce a high Two Pair. Such a two card draw also has a bluff value, as opponents may think the player holds Three of a Kind.

Drawing two cards to an open-end Straight Flush ♦: Q,,J,10 — offers about 1 out of 12 chances of making a Straight or a Flush, with a Straight Flush a very remote prospect.

A One Card Draw is the only way of improving Two Pair. It allows about a 1 out of 12 chance of making a Full House.

With four parts toward an open-end Straight — 10 ♥, 9 ♦, 8 ♦, 7 ♣ — a player has 1 out of 6 chances of *filling* the Straight — J, 10, 9, 8, 7 or 10, 9, 8, 7, 6 — so it is often worthwhile. An *inside* Straight — Q♠, J♣, 10♠, 8♥ — offers only 1 out of 12 chances, so is rarely worth the try.

A *Four Flush* with four cards of the same suit — ♦: Q, 9, 7, 3 — is a better bet than an *open-end* Straight, as the chance of catching a fifth card is 1 out of 5, and a Flush beats a Straight.

Many players draw only one card when holding Three of a Kind. The chance of improving is about 1 out of 12, almost as good as a two card draw. Drawing one card makes the hand look like Two Pair, or a possible Straight or Flush, which may fool an opponent into betting badly.

With Four of a Kind, a player often draws one card for similar reasons, as it looks as though he is trying to improve a hand which is actually as good as it can be.

Standing Pat is necessary with a Straight, a Flush, a Full House, or a Straight Flush, as the player has no card that he can throw away. It is often advisable to stand pat on Four of a Kind, as opponents may think the hand is in a lesser category.

Occasionally, a player will stand pat on Two Pair, figuring that it makes his hand look stronger, and that the chance of getting a Full House from a one card draw is too small to matter.

Bluffing may be carried to any extreme a player wants. He can stand pat on a *nothing* hand if he thinks it will scare other players into dropping out. The bigger the stakes, the more the chance to bluff, as a hand looks strong when backed with plenty of chips.

Limits are customary in the great majority of Poker games, so a player must bet accordingly. Usually two amounts are stated, as 5-10 or 5-25, which may refer to chips, cents, dollars, or *what have you*. The first figure represents the lowest bet; the last figure, the highest.

Usually, the first figure is also the ante. So in *Five-Ten* Poker, each player would put up 5 units, except in games where the dealer antes for all, that being a simpler way to handle it. In the play, each person would bet or raise either 5 or 10 units, as inbetween amounts — 5, 6, 7, 8, 9 — are inconvenient. In some, as *Five-Twenty-five*, bets and raises would run 5, 10, 15, 20, 25.

Sometimes only the minimum bet is allowed before the draw, and this has led to the fixing of three units, as 5-10-25, meaning that the game is 5-10 before the draw, and 10-25 afterward. If desired, it can be 5-10 before and 5-25 after. All these things are fixed by agreement.

About the cheapest form of Poker is *penny ante*, which operates on a 1¢ basis, pennies often being used instead of chips. In some games, everyone antes 1 penny and the limits are 1¢ to 5¢, with anything in between. In contrast, some groups play 1 to 5 or 1 to 10 with dollars as the units instead of cents. Poker is that flexible.

Roodles, also known as *Whangdoodles,* is a term referring to a round of play at double stakes, or more. Often, by agreement, this follows any hand won by a Full House or better, such a hand being popularly styled a whangdoodle. The round consists of a deal by every player until it reaches the one who dealt the whangdoodle. The roodles end before his deal.

Jackpots or Jacks or Better

Jackpots, also called Jacks or Better, is the form of Draw Poker favored in most circles. In such a game, a player must have at least a Pair of Jacks in order to open. If he drops or wins the hand without opposition, he must show a pair of Jacks or something better, to prove he had openers.

Sometimes a player *splits* his openers, say by discarding a King from a Pair, in order to go after a higher hand like a Straight or Flush. So he should keep his discard handy, to show his openers if required.

Since a Pair of Jacks is a better than average hand, there are times when nobody can open, so the deal moves along. This requires another ante, increasing the size of the pot. Players are not compelled to open, so a player *under the guns* at the dealer's left may sometimes throw in a hand containing a Pair of Jacks, or even a higher Pair.

All this swells the pot with further antes, which is the main purpose of Jackpots. If so agreed, the rule can be made *progressive*. After passing a hand, the next requires a Pair of Queens or better, then Kings, and finally Aces. The requirement can even be pushed up to Two Pair, if desired. Most groups, however, prefer to stay with simple Jackpots.

In games where a player can open on anything, some groups go by the rule that a player must open or drop, rather than being allowed to pass and come back later. In Jackpots, the rule of *pass and back in* is customary. Thus, any player is able to stay in the face of Jacks or Better, regardless of his position at the table.

Styles of Play in Draw Poker

Taking Jacks or Better as the most popular form of Draw Poker, you will find that the styles of play vary widely, accord-

16

ing to the types of players and the betting limits of the game. All are confronted by the same three questions — but from there on, opinions differ. The three questions are:

1) when to open the pot
2) when to stay
3) when to raise

In a sociable, low-limit game, those questions are easily answered. The first player who holds a Pair of Jacks will open automatically. Anyone holding any kind of a Pair will stay. With four parts toward a Straight or Flush, all will either stay or raise. With anything higher than a Pair, most are apt to raise. In a steeper game, inexperienced players often follow this same procedure, and are generally dim-witted enough to wonder why they become heavy losers.

The most glaring error is to stay on a low Pair. In so doing, a player figures that if he can catch a third card to go with his Pair of Sevens, or whatever he is holding, he will beat any bigger Pair that the opener may hold, like Jacks, Queens, Kings or Aces. Also, he can win if he picks up a second pair, to give himself Two Pair — as Sevens over Fives. He may realize that the odds are 2½ to 1 against him, where improving his hand is concerned, but he takes the risk, thinking that if he does improve, he can raise the opener's next bet and win that much more.

He can raise, all right, but he can't be sure of a win, because the opener has an equal chance of improving his hand along the same lines, and if he does, he will be the winner. For example: Player "A" opens on a Pair of Kings, while Player "B" stays on a Pair of Eights. Both draw three cards; if each gets two Fives, A will have Two Pair, Kings over Fives, which beat B's Eights over Fives. If each draws a third card to his Pair, A's Three Kings will ruin B's Three Eights.

Hence no smart player will stay on less than a Pair of Jacks, except under special circumstances. Sometimes a player is tempted to stay on a Pair of Tens, thinking they are "almost as good'' as Jacks. But they might just as well be a Pair of Threes, if you are bucking a Pair of Jacks on your own. However, in a loose, low-limit game, where as many as four players will stay on a low Pair, a player with a Pair of Tens is well off if he catches his third Ten, because his Three of a Kind will top any lesser Three of a Kind, if another player makes one.

Assuming, however, that everybody is reasonably smart, it would be simple indeed for a player to open on a Pair of Jacks and pick up the pot, consisting of the *ante,* when all the other players drop. But suppose one other player stays; and when the opener draws three cards, the other player does the same. The opener, knowing that his opponent is smart, immediately realizes that he is up against a higher Pair — Queens, Kings or Aces — and therefore is in the same position as a player with a low Pair. So being smart, he should drop. But his opponent, also being smart, might be just wise enough to stay on a low Pair, or even a nothing hand, just to bluff the opener into quitting cold.

This simply shows how the player who calculates mathematically can be outwitted by one who calculates psychologically, although that, too, can work in reverse. But the upshot is this: keen Jackpot players refuse to be caught in such a bind. So, they follow this rule: don't open on a Pair of Jacks, unless you are the dealer and everybody else has passed. In a six player game, if you are the first or second man to the dealer's left, don't open with less than a Pair of Aces, or perhaps a Pair of Kings. If you are number three or four, make it a Pair of Kings or Queens. If five or six, a Pair of Jacks will do, though it would be nicer with a Pair of Queens.

In any case, the whole idea is to *steal the pot,* which consists of the ante. To clarify this: in a Five and Ten game — which can mean five and ten cents, five and ten dollars, fifty and a hundred dollars, and so on — six players have put in five units each, making thirty units in the pot. So Player A opens with a Pair of Jacks for five, giving the pot a total of thirty-five, which he will win if nobody stays. So Player B stays for five — a chance of one in seven that he can improve his hand sufficiently to beat Player A. That is justifiable as good mathematics, but not as good Poker.

In good Poker, B might let A take the pot, but so reluctantly that A would remember it. Then, if the situation arose again, B would raise A with anything — or nothing — hoping that A would drop. This is especially true when a double pot is at stake. For example: Six players put in an ante of five units each, a total of thirty. Cards are dealt and nobody has Jacks or Better. So the deal moves on and everybody *antes* five units more, putting sixty in the pot. This time, Player A opens for five units, the limit in the first betting round, making a total of sixty-five units, in the pot. For a mere five units, Player B can stay on a Pair of Sixes, figuring that the odds of getting Three of a Kind are about equal to those offered by the pot, roughly one in twelve.

This shows the flexibility of the game and offers a recommended formula some players have used with good results. That is to open the pot whenever you can, even if you are among the first three players in a table of six and have only a Pair of Jacks. In that case, if anybody else stays, you draw only two cards to make them think that you opened with Three of a Kind. It's good if you have an Ace or King to go with a Pair of Jacks or Queens, but a lower card like a Seven or Eight will do, because even though you're bluffing, Two Pair may be all you need to win.

If you actually have Two Pair, open with them. Here, some players hold back, hoping somebody else will open and if nobody does, the Two Pair are a total loss. So it's better to open with them and if a few other players stay, treat your Two Pair as though they were a *pat hand,* like a Straight, Flush or Full House. Don't draw any cards at all, just sit tight. This applies particularly with a high Two Pair — Aces, Kings or even Queens up — and also when most of the other players have already passed. If an earlier player comes in with a small Pair and makes Three of a Kind, or goes for a low Straight and fills it, your *pat hand* may scare him into dropping out. Also, if some player thinks you're bluffing and tries to get by with Two Pair of his own, yours will probably top his.

By the same token, if you have a low Two Pair — like Sixes over Fours — and are in the first, second or even third slot, it can be smart to pass, as many players do with Two Pair. But in your case, there will be a special purpose. You draw one card, which is a standard draw in this case, because you are hoping to turn your low Two Pair into a Full House. Example: You hold **6♣, 6♥, 3♥, 3♦, 10♠**. You discard the **10♠**, hoping to draw a Six or a Three to fill your Full House, as 6,6,6,3,3 or 3,3,3,6,6. It's a long shot — only about one chance in twelve — still it's worth a try in case the opener, coming in with a high Pair, such as Kings, should hook a high Two Pair that would beat your low Two Pair (as K,K,4,4 vs. 6,6,3,3.)

That, however, is only half the story. By laying back instead of opening, you are able to raise the player who does open, which immediately gives your hand a strong significance. The fact that you passed implies that you were unable to open; and when you draw one card, you must be going after a Straight or a Flush, because of your raise. After the draw, if the opener checks, you promptly bet. If he should bet, you raise. Either way, opponents are apt to figure that you filled your Straight or Flush; and that could cause the opener or others to drop with Two Pair, Three of a Kind or even a small Straight.

Note that this is not a case of outright bluff, since bluffing is generally regarded as betting on a hand that you think is due to lose. Here, you may be counting on your Two Pair to win, on the assumption none of the other players had better than a high Pair to start and that they, too, failed to improve their hands. Thus, if the opener calls you with his Pair of Kings, thinking that you were bluffing with a Four Flush, he will find that you had him beaten all along and were simply hoping for a Full

House to clinch it.

Even if you lose, a hand like this is helpful because in the showdown, people see that you were betting on something solid. But to put real teeth into this gimmick, you should occasionally raise on a high Bobtail Straight or a Four Flush and advertise the fact. If you miss, you promptly toss in your hand, letting other players see it if they want, to leave no doubt that you are after a Straight or Flush. It so happens that most experts advise against even staying on a Bobtail Straight or Four Flush, unless practically all the other players have already stayed, because your chance of filling is only one in six with a Straight and one in five with a Flush. So if only three or four players stay, you will lose more pots than you win; and there is no percentage in that.

True enough, but Straights in general and Flushes in particular are the kind of hands that take big pots, as they give you opportunities to raise and thereby win bigger pots. Furthermore, once people realize that you raise on prospects of a Straight or Flush, you will get results when you raise with Two Pair and draw one card, as already recommended. Also, if somebody opens ahead of you when you have been dealt Three of a Kind, you can raise and make a one card draw, holding a *kicker* with your *Trips,* again making them think that you have filled a Straight or Flush when you bet the limit.

When opening with a Three of a Kind, it is also good policy to hold a *kicker,* because since you can't open with a Bobtail or a Four Flush, people will suppose that you hold Two Pair. Almost any player with a high Two Pair — as Aces or Kings up — will be sure to bet against you, only to lose out. The higher your Three of a Kind the better, because anyone with low Triplets is apt to raise you, thinking you only have Two Pair.

Use of the suggestions so far given hinges greatly upon the type of players in your group and the size of the stakes involved. When most of the players stay on anything once the pot is opened, you can afford to take a few risks yourself, rather than be branded as a *tight* player. However, you may find it easier to bluff certain players when you are in that category, because they will think that unless your hand is an almost sure winner, you wouldn't be betting at all. However, in high limit games, there are many players who wait for a Full House or Four of a Kind, hoping some opponent will have a hand only a shade lower, so they can raise and reraise and wind up with a big killing.

Some players swear by a long-established rule of never opening on less than Three of a Kind. By the same token, they should never stay on anything else, because if all the players followed that rule, they would need Three of a Kind or better to win. So in actuality, such a game, instead of being Jacks or Better would become Trips or Better. The trouble with this system is that you have about one chance in fifty of getting Three of a Kind before the draw, so in a six-handed game, more than half-a-dozen deals may pass before Three of a Kind shows up and by then, the *antes* would swell the pot to such proportions that it would be worth opening on a Pair of Jacks and staying on anything — even an Ace-King or a Three Flush.

So if you try the Trips or Better system, you should at least disregard it when pots begin to pile up; occasionally open on something less and advertise the fact, to keep people from knowing how faithful you are to Trips or Better. One good way to handle this is to open with a Pair of Jacks or a higher Pair when you also have four parts toward a Straight or a Flush. You can then split your openers by discarding a Jack and going for the Straight or Flush, as the case may be. Later, you show your discarded Jack to prove you had openers.

Some specialists in Jackpots are prompt to open with a Pair of Aces, although they would ordinarily hold back on an average Two Pair or even low Triplets. They look at it this way: if the Pair of Aces does not improve, they can still beat any other high Pair, except possibly another Pair of Aces. If they catch a

22

smaller Pair to go with them, they should beat any other Two Pair. If they get a third Ace, they have the next best thing to a Straight. Instead of drawing three cards, they may hold a high *kicker* and draw two to make it look like Trips to start.

Even players who ordinarily refuse to draw one card toward a Straight or Flush should stay and preferably raise with four parts toward a Straight Flush, which offers as many as 15 out of 47 chances of a fill, or close to one out of three. Even with only an inside Straight — as ♥ : **J, 10, 9, 7** — it offers 12 out of 47, or about one out of four. That should satisfy the most discriminating percentage player.

Opening on Anything

As opposed to Jackpots, many groups of players revert to the older form of Draw Poker in which no openers are required. This has an important bearing on the game for various reasons. It is usually played on the basis that a player must bet or drop, and in this form is popularly known as Pass-out. This prevents a player from laying back with a strong hand and then raising the others after someone else has opened. Conversely, a player does not have to reveal that he has Jacks or Better when he opens.

This encourages a player to go after a Straight or a Flush, as he can open just as readily with a Bobtail or a Four Flush as he would with Two Pair. Players often open or stay with a small Pair and particularly a small Pair with an Ace or King as kicker since they are not faced by the threat of opposing Jacks. Thus if the first few players pass, it's a pretty sure thing that a small Pair has a big chance; even those who do open may be figuring the same way. The bad point is that this makes players overly optimistic. If you are sure that there will be three others staying in the deal, you will do well to stick with Jacks or Better, so far as a Pair is concerned.

After the draw, everybody must bet or drop, beginning with the opener. Since the opener can't check, this makes it all the easier to get by with something like a Pair of Tens, or even a Pair of Nines, or even less. This, however, makes a high Bobtail Straight a real good bet. Suppose you hold K ♥, Q ♦, J ♥, 10♣. You have eight chances of catching an Ace or Nine for a Straight — A,K,Q,J,10 or K,Q,J,10,9 — for a sure win; but in addition, you have *twelve chances* of catching *any* King, Queen, Jack or Ten, which may beat a couple of low Pair hands, or unfilled Straights or Flushes.

If you choose, this game can be played like Jackpots, letting players pass and come back in before the draw; allowing a player to check after the draw by putting the betting privilege up to the next man. In that case, the game is popularly termed Pass and Back In. There used to be an old saying, ''You pay your money and take your choice.'' In this case, it should be, ''You take your choice and pay your money.''

In this form, the game is technically termed Straight Poker. It allows for a little more finesse or skullduggery, whichever you want to term it, but it amounts to about the same in the long run.

Blind Opening

This is the big action game of the high bettors. It is played with various rules that can be changed or modified according to the purposes, desires or whims of the participants. In every form, the first player to the dealer's left is forced to open *blind:* that is, make a bet without looking at his hand. From there on, the procedure can be normal, with players doing as they please; or the next player is forced to *straddle,* by doubling the opener's bet — also without looking at his hand. This naturally increases the action appreciably and as if that were not enough, a further rule may be agreed upon.

That is, *allowing* the third player to straddle by doubling the

24

second player's bet, and — if so agreed beforehand — the fourth player be *allowed* to do the same thing. Usually after the third player, the privilege is curtailed; and certainly it should be after the fourth player. In any event, once the straddling is ended either voluntarily or by rule, the next player can look at his hand and decide whether or not he wants to stay.

If he decides to stay, he must meet the last straddler's bet; or, if so agreed, he must double it.

From then on, each player can look at his hand and stay for that same amount; or he can drop or raise, whichever he chooses. When the betting gets around to the first player, or the *blind* as he is known, he can look at his hand and decide whether he wants to stay, drop or raise; the same applies to each of the *straddlers* as the next players in rotation are termed.

After all who stay have equalized their bets, the players draw, beginning to the dealer's left. The first player to the left of the last *straddler* starts the betting, being regarded as the opener; providing he is still in the game. If not, the man to his left opens, and so on. Betting continues as in standard Draw Poker, except that each player must bet, call, raise or drop; no *checking* to the next player is permitted in this game, unless by agreement.

The number of straddles, the forced bets and raises, as well as the betting limits, can be decided by the group itself. The limit following the draw can be set beforehand. For example, if the *blind* is compelled to bet one chip to start, the limit after the draw can be four times that amount; in this case, four chips. Another plan is to make it double the amount by which the last *straddler* raised during the early betting round.

Freak hands, such as Blazes, Dogs, Cats and any others have a place in this game, as they encourage players to straddle on the chance of picking up some lucky combination or making an equally lucky draw. The game can be played with or without an *ante*, but is usually played without one. For that reason Blind Opening is sometimes termed Blind Ante, but this is somewhat a misnomer, as the compulsory contribution by the *blind* is more in the nature of a bet than an ante.

III

STUD POKER

In contrast to Draw Poker, in which no player sees another's cards until the showdown, there is a popular form called Stud Poker in which the majority of the cards are dealt face up. Thus, giving players a chance to appraise rival hands during the deal, which is halted at intervals to allow the players to bet on their comparative prospects. For this reason, Draw Poker is termed Closed Poker because a player keeps his cards closed from view, while Stud Poker is known as Open Poker because some of a player's cards are openly shown.

Actually, Stud is a much keener and more skillful game than Draw, though superficially it would seem the other way around. Even in the basic form of Five Card Stud, in which four of a player's five cards are dealt face up, so much can hinge on the lone face-down card that big-time players have been known to bluff one another for gigantic pots. The same applies to the Seven Card version, in which three cards are face-down and four face-up, as well as countless variants of Stud.

Hence, many Poker lovers became annoyed when the state of California declared Poker to be a legal game, but only in the form of Draw, not Stud. It is indeed quite ludicrous that the more skillful game should still be outlawed while the less skill-ful game is regularly played in licensed betting parlors. But there is a point that has been somewhat overlooked in this regard; namely, in Draw Poker, a player is never a sure winner until the showdown. Even if he holds a Royal Flush, another player can match it to tie the hand. But in Stud Poker, a player with an Ace face-up and another face-down is a sure winner over a rival whose face-up cards show nothing higher than a King. No amount of skill can win over such a setup!

Five Card Stud

This is the original form of Stud Poker from which several other versions have developed. Ordinarily, there is no ante in Five Card Stud, though this is optional. In Stud, all cards are kept on the table. As many as ten players can participate comfortably in Five Card Stud.

Two cards are dealt to each player, a *hole card,* face down, and an *up card,* face up. Each player is allowed to look at his hole card. The player with the highest up card must either open or drop, which in Stud is called *folding* because he turns down his up card. If two players are tied for high card, the one nearest to the dealer's left must open, or fold. If he drops out, then it is up to the next man to his left to open, no matter how low an up card he shows.

Once the pot is opened, succeeding players can fold, call or raise. This continues until all have either folded or called. A third card is then dealt to all the players who have stayed. Again, the player with the highest up card bets first, but now he may be showing a Pair, rather than just a high card. Also, he may check on the third card, instead of betting.

In that case, succeeding players may also check or bet. If he bets, they may either call, raise or fold. After all have called or folded, a fourth card is dealt to all who are still in the hand. The same procedure follows, but this time, it is possible for the high player to be showing Three of a Kind.

A fifth card is then dealt. Again, the player with the best up card is the first to speak. After all best evened, the players who have stayed turn up their hole cards. The best hand wins. Often, competition is keen up to the fifth and final card.

From the time when Five Card Stud surged to popularity, keen followers of the game began looking for ways to make the most of their holdings with a minimum chance of loss. At that time, the term Stud Poker meant the five card game, since no other rivaled it until the mid-1920s. Five Card Stud still continued to be popular, but with rivals in the field, the quest for a sure winning system became all the more urgent, in order to keep players from jumping to innovative games like Seven Card Stud and its variants.

While an infallible formula was impossible, experts in Five Card Stud at least approached it with a safe way system that was both simple and effective. It consisted of eight words easily remembered, furnishing advice that, if followed to the letter, would so protect a player against loss that he could almost bank on being a winner after a prolonged session — the only question being how big his gain might be.

That catch-phrase was: *Fold if you are beaten on the board*.

By the rules of Five Card Stud then in vogue, and which still apply among serious groups, there is no ante in Five Card Stud. It means that a player could sit in on a game all night, turning down his first two cards on every deal, without ever putting a chip into the pot. That would be a very good way to study the other players and learn their styles of play, in order to take advantage of them at some future session. But to sit back and do nothing would only invite suspicion, so it is absolutely essential to show some sign of action.

That can be done with the Safe Way System.

First, let us define the term *beaten on the board*. This means that on the initial deal, one of your two cards — the hole card or the up card — must be as high in value as any other player's up card, unless your first two cards happen to form a Pair, which naturally beats any lone card that is showing on the board. As each succeeding card is dealt, you study the opposing up cards on the same basis, folding if you are beaten on the board. The only difference is that the situation becomes more involved as the deal progresses.

As a compact illustration, suppose that you are dealt the **Q♣** as a hole card, with the **9♠** as an up card, so that your holding is **(Q♣) 9♠**. The highest up card in sight is the **K♦**. So you fold, because your Queen-high is beaten by a King-high, even though your **Q♣** may be higher than six other up cards showing on the board. In contrast, let's suppose that the highest rival up card was only the **J♦**. In that case, you would stay. So let's consider it on that basis.

Suppose your next up card is the **10♣**, giving you **(Q♣) 9♠, 10♣**. Unfortunately, your opponent, who was dealt the **J♦**, happens to get the **Q♥**, giving him *J♦, Q♥. This means that you must fold, because your hand only rates Q,10,9, whereas his hand, judged from his up cards, is headed by a Queen-Jack.

Again, as a contrast, suppose your opponent was dealt a lower third card — the **6♣**, so your hand would stand **(Q♣), 9♠, 10♣** against his *J♦, 6♣. Your Q,10,9 is higher than his Jack-Six, so of course, you stay. Suppose that by then, everyone else has dropped, so you and your lone rival are each dealt a fourth card, and you find to your annoyance that he is not dead yet; but you are. Even though you are dealt the **K♣**, he happens to get the **6♠**, so your hands stand:

Yours: **(Q♣), 9♠, 10♣, K♦**   *His:* *J♦, 6♣, 6♠

As promising as your hand looks, your K, Q, 10, 9 is beaten on the board by his Pair of Sixes, so in conformity to the Safe Way System, you must fold, letting him take the pot without bothering to complete the hands with the deal of a fifth card each. Actually, you are playing it safe, because there are four chances out of a possible thirteen that if you were dealt another card, it would give you a pair higher than your opponent's Sixes. Those values are King, Queen, Ten and Nine. But if your opponent has almost the same chance of either getting a third Six, or matching up one of his first two cards (his hole card and up card) to give him a winning Two Pair (as J,J,6,6). A Jack would give you a Straight (K,Q,J,10,9) but that still only gives you five possible values out of thirteen, though your Straight would be a winner, even if your opponent made Two Pair or Three of a Kind.

You may ask, "Just how much did the Safe Way System help me, considering that I lost, anyway?"

The answer is, "You can't win them all, but you can put yourself in line for a win, which you did in this case. You also saved any bet you might have wasted on a fifth card, since the odds that it would bring you a win were about 2 to 1 against you."

The system, however, goes deeper than that. Since you have to have what could be the best hand in order to stay, people recognize that and are apt to respect you. So if you decide to bluff, which is an important phase of Poker, especially when the stakes are steep, you are in a position to do so. In this case, a bluff in the form of a limit bet might have served you well. If your hole card happened to be a Nine, you would have the edge on your opponent, unless he, too, happened to have a potent hole card, say a Jack. Often, a study of up cards held by other players, while they were still showing, can be the determining factor when it comes to a question of bluff.

The Safe Way System has still another vital point in its favor. Assuming that your opponent was also using it, in his case, the system brought him home as winner. Also, if the other players were using the system, it was the reason why they dropped out early, thereby avoiding any loss, or at least keeping their losses at a minimum.

Now that you understand the Safe Way System, with its one vital rule, *"Fold when you are beaten on the board,"* you can study its details in the illustrative deal given on the opposite page. There, all eight players, with one exception — Player "A" — followed the Safe Way System.

Analysis of Safe Way System

1st Two Cards

Players:	"A"	"B"	"C"	"D"	"E"	"F"	"G"	"H"
Hole Card:	(K♠)	(5♣)	(Q♠)	(4♠)	(7♦)	(2♣)	(A♠)	(3♣)
Up Card:	10♥	2♠	Q♦	4♣	7♥	3♠	J♦	5♦

Analysis: When "C" opens with his high Q♦, Players "F," "H," and "B" drop out because they are *beaten on the board*. The following players stay, because each has a higher holding than the Q♦: Player "D" stays with his Pair of Fours; "E" with his Pair of Sevens; "G" with his A♠ in the hole; and "A" with his K♠ in the hole. So there are five live players on the next deal.

3rd Card

	"A"	"C"	"D"	"E"	"G"
Hole Card:	(K♠)	(Q♠)	(4♠)	(7♦)	(A♠)
2nd Up:	10♥	Q♦	4♣	7♥	J♦
3rd Up:	J♣	K♥	10♣	9♥	5♠

Analysis: Here, "A" should drop, because his King-Jack is beaten by "C's" King-Queen. "D" and "E" stay, because each has a Pair; and "G," with Ace-high also stays. But it happens that "A" did stay, regardless of the system.

4th Card

	"A"	"C"	"D"	"E"	"G"
Hole Card:	(K♠)	(Q♠)	(4♠)	(7♦)	(A♠)
2nd Up:	10♥	Q♦	4♣	7♥	J♦
3rd Up:	J♣	K♥	10♣	9♥	5♠
4th Up:	8♣	7♠	8♦	4♦	A♦

Analysis: "A" has still less excuse for staying, as his King-Jack is topped by "G" with Ace-Jack and "D" with

King-Queen. Still he stays, like "D" and "E" who have a right to do so.

Final Card	"A"	"C"	"D"	"E"	"G"
Hole Card:	(K♠)	(Q♠)	(4♠)	(7♦)	(A♠)
2nd Up:	10♥	Q♦	4♣	7♠	J♦
3rd Up:	J♣	K♥	10♣	9♥	5♠
4th Up:	8♣	7♠	8♦	4♦	A♦
5th Up:	J♠	4♥	7♣	K♣	6♠

Analysis: "G," with his Ace in the hole, knows he is a sure winner with a Pair of Aces and bets accordingly.

Player "A" was included to show how a player can encounter problems when everyone else is playing safe. From the start, "A" should have realized that at least three players — "D," "E" and "G" — must have had an Ace, King or Queen in the hole, or a Pair *back to back* in order to match the Q♦ that Player "C" showed as his up card.

However, "A" was reasonably justified in staying after the third card was dealt, since if the K♥ was of no value to "C" as was quite likely, the status of the other players remained unchanged. The J♣ dealt to "A" was better than anything that came their way and it gave him three parts to a Straight — K-J-10 — which at least deserved consideration. However, with the fourth card, it became pretty obvious that "A" was beaten since his chance for a Straight was gone; and "G", who was dealt an Ace, promptly bet after "C" and the others checked.

Players "C", "D" and "E" all had a right to stay for the last card which might have given any of them Two Pair or Three of a Kind, which made it all the more hopeless for "A". But when "G" won with a Pair of Aces, over "C", who had a Pair of Queens all along, all that "A" could have hoped for was a King, instead of "G" getting an Ace, which would have made him the winner. As it was, he did pair up his Jacks, which still weren't good enough to match the Pair of Queens held by "C". This simply illustrates the fallacy of over-estimating the possibilities of a hand.

Now that we have extolled the Safe Way System, let's consider it from other angles. First, if everybody followed the system, the game could frequently become dull and sometimes pointless. For example, if only one Ace appeared among the original up cards and nobody happened to have an Ace in the hole, with no Pairs back to back, everybody would fold except the player with the Ace. If the highest up card happened to be a King, Queen, or even a Jack, with nobody having anything better, the same rule would apply.

Yet here it could be very sensible to stay, as the chance of the player with the high up card having a back to back Pair is only three out of thirty-eight in a seven-player game, making it about one out of twelve. As another example, suppose the first player showed an Ace as up card and the next stayed with a Three as up card. The other players then drop until it comes to you. You have the Q♠ showing and the J♠ as your hole card. So why should you drop? There are six cards — three Jacks, three Queens — that will give you a higher Pair than Threes, while the player with the Ace as an up card will probably have to hook another Ace to beat your prospective pair of Queens or Jacks.

What's more, your Q♠ and J♠ represent two parts toward a Straight and a Flush. Though chances of making one or the other are very slight, they still represent possibilities that can only be realized if you keep your hand alive and see what turns up. So the overall advice is to stay for another card, or maybe two, particularly when the limit is low, so the risk you take is not too costly.

That brings up two other points. One is the matter of the ante. In modern games like Dealer's Choice, where the dealer can call for Stud instead of Draw, an ante is customary when Stud is chosen. So you can't sit out a round of Five Card Stud without paying for the privilege. Since you have to pay, you may as well play; and when several players adopt that way of thinking, the game loosens up. If you can spot the *tight* players, it should be reasonably safe to stay whenever they fold, as you will be up against softer competition.

This leads to what might be termed the One Ahead System.

Here, if your first two cards show any possibilities, you stay, even though the board shows you beaten. Low cards are all right, if they might lead to a Straight, a Flush, or preferably both. The real crux comes with the third card. If nobody pairs up and your hand still shows good prospects, you stay. Even if somebody does catch a Pair on the board, you keep thinking of the next card to come. If it will give you a higher Pair than the one showing on the board, you stay. That's why it's called the One Ahead.

Take this deal as a good example:

Players:	"A"	"B"	"C"	"D"	"E"	"F"	"G"
Hole Card	(4♣)	(3♥)	(Q♠)	(9♦)	(10♠)	(8♠)	(6♠)
2nd Up	5♦	10♥	K♦	8♣	7♥	J♥	2♠
3rd Up	9♣	A♥	K♣	Q♥	K♠	8♥	9♠
4th Up	—	K♠	3♠	6♣	—	J♦	7♦
5th Up	—	2♣	5♣	—	—	4♦	—

In a tight game, with everybody following the Safe Way System, only Player "C" would have stayed, since his K♦ was higher than anything else. But by the One Ahead, all had prospects at that time. "A" had two parts toward a Straight, 4♣ and 5♦. "B" had two parts toward a Heart Flush. "C" was not only high, but had two parts to a Straight, Q♠ and K♦. "D" had two parts toward a Straight, 9♦ and 8♣. So did "E" with 10♠, 7♥ and "F" with 8♠ and J♥. "G", with 6♠ and 2♠, had two parts toward a Straight Flush.

With the third card, Player "C" caught a Pair of Kings, which would have scared everyone off if they were playing it the Safe Way. But with the One Ahead, it added up thus: "D" stayed on the possibility of a Queen-high Straight. "E" folded as his chance for a Straight was gone and there was only one King left to pair up with his **K ♥**. "F" stayed, because he had a Pair of Eights and though there was only one Eight left that would give him Triplets, there were three Jacks loose that would be good for Two Pair, J,J,8,8. "G" stayed, with three Spades toward a Flush. "A" folded, because he had nothing high enough to beat a Pair of Kings on the next card and the **9♣** killed his chance of a Straight. "B" stayed in hope of hitting a Pair of Aces on his fourth or fifth card, as he had the only Ace showing on the board and also three parts toward a Heart Flush.

With the fourth card, "C" checked with his Pair of Kings, for it was obvious now that he could not get a third, since all four were on the board. "D" folded as the **6♣** killed his chance for a Straight and made it impossible for him to get a high enough Pair to win. "F" stayed with his **J ♦** which gave him a Pair of Jacks showing on the board. "G" folded since the **7 ♦** killed his chance for a Spade Flush, which he would need in order to win. "B" stayed, still hoping for another Ace.

Nobody improved on the final card, with the result that Player "F" won with his Two Pair (J,J,8,8) over Player "B" with his Pair of Kings. All the rest felt that they were justified in staying as long as they did, although Player "B" admitted later that he was on the point of folding when Player "F" hooked the **J ♦**, as it looked as though "F" might have Three Jacks, since none were showing on the board. But "B" still felt that a Pair of Aces would almost surely beat "C's" Pair of Kings, which looked like the big threat, so "B" decided to stay. His one consolation was that an Ace wouldn't have helped him anyway.

This shows how far players can go when thinking in terms of One Ahead as opposed to the Safe Way. Obviously, a keen player who can size up his opponents should find a middle course highly profitable. In a reasonably loose game, there is no reason to pass up opportunities by playing too safe, but it is equally unwise to stay too long in the face of increasing opposition.

Six Card Stud

This is a very remarkable outgrowth of Five Card Stud. Those who play Six card Stud regularly regard it as the best of Poker games. They base this on the fact that interest fades in a Five Card game, when one hand is far too good in comparison with the other, which is often true.

So Six Card Stud was invented. It calls for the dealing of a sixth card, face down, which becomes an alternate card, replacing any card of the original five. There is an extra betting round on the sixth card, and with each player having two hole cards, the betting is apt to prove much stronger.

As a variation, some groups have the sixth card dealt as an up card. This is a good game, too, but it tends to lessen the suspense, as five cards are actually showing, and might form a Straight, Flush or Full House, which would kill any other visible hand.

Seven Card Stud

This game, popularly known as Down the River and Seven Card Pete, has practically come to dominate the Stud situation. It is one step beyond the six card game, and puts the probabilities of Draw into Stud. This makes it the ideal form of Poker, in the estimate of many players. The procedure is as follows.

Three cards are dealt to each player. Two are down cards or hole cards. The third is an up card and the players bet it exactly as in Five Card Stud. That constitutes the first betting round. The highest card showing — nearest to the dealer in case of a tie — must make a bet or fold.

37

A fourth card is dealt to each player. Now, the high hand can either check or bet. The same applies to a fifth card and a sixth, each being dealt face up. The seventh card is dealt face down, and another round of betting follows. After all the remaining players call, the hole cards are turned up and the player showing the best five cards wins.

To recap. Rounds of betting follow the deal of the 3rd, 4th, 5th, 6th, and 7th cards. At the finish, three cards are down and four are up. Thus the players do not show their complete hands until all bets are called.

There is one important point to remember. In Draw or Five Card Stud, the hands are self-evident and must be judged accordingly. But in Seven Card Stud, they go according to the player's own declaration. If he holds a hand such as: K♠, Q♦, J♦, 10♥, 9♦, 5♦, 3♦ he might call it a King-high Straight — K, Q, J, 10, 9 — by discarding the 5♦ and 3♦. But he would do better to call it a Diamond Flush — ♦: Q,J,9,5,3 — and throw out the K♠ and 10♥.

When to "Stay" in Seven Card Stud

In Seven Card Stud, much depends on the first three cards. Unless you have something to start with, you're not apt to have anything worthwhile at the finish. There are some optimistic players who argue otherwise, but the law of averages is against them. They look at it this way. If you take three Aces, shuffle them in with four odd cards and deal them out, you will still have three Aces, regardless of the order in which they turn up.

That is very true, but the rule doesn't hold with seven cards taken at random, since there is no guarantee that three Aces will be among them. Surprises do pop up in the final cards of a seven deal, but not as often as some people think. They are inclined to remember such hands and overlook those that turned out to be a total bust. So a hand that starts out with good cards is really the only type of hand to play.

That raises the question, just how good should the first three cards be? That depends to some degree on whether the game has a high or low limit, as well as the type of players involved. With a lot at stake, you should naturally be careful about choosing starters; but in a social game, you can afford to be more liberal. Keep this in mind — if you play a *tight* game when everybody else is taking chances, some of your best hands may lose out, because of the chance of surprise hands cropping up. So you might as well get in the swim yourself, though not too deeply.

Since we have mentioned Three Aces, we may as well mark it as the ideal holding to start off a hand of Seven Card Stud. With two Aces as hole cards and an a third as an up card, you are likely to have the pot won then and there, since the average winning hand in Seven Card Stud is probably around Three Nines. The presence of an Ace as an up card does not give away the fact that you have two others in the hole; in fact, it may create the impression that your other cards are not too good and that you are counting on a lone Ace to bolster them. However, by the time five or six cards have been dealt, with no Aces appearing among them, other players may suspect that your hand is better than they thought.

Taking Three Aces as the best possible starter, it follows that Three Kings will come next, then Three Queens and so on down the scale. The general groupings are:

Any Three of a Kind: The higher the trio the better, not only because it may win over another set of Triplets, but because high cards are logical to hold. When you get down to a Five or lower as your initial up card, people may wonder why you are staying with it, unless later up cards make them think that you are going for a Straight or a Flush. Unless you find yourself practically beaten on the board, stay with those Trips to the bitter end. Remember that when you have Triplets to start, any Pair will give you a Full House; and chances of making a

"Full" are usually good right up to the seventh card.

Three to a Straight Flush: This type of hand is loaded with prospects which should never be ignored. You don't get it often, but when you do, you have up to a 40% chance of hitting a Straight or a Flush for a very likely win; and such hands are hard to make without strong help to start. The ideal setup consists of three high cards of the same suit in sequence, with a combination like ♥ : Q, J, 10 rating as the best. This gives you a chance of filling with the following combinations: any Ace and King; any King and Nine; or any Nine and Eight for a Straight. Also, any two Hearts out of a possible ten make a Flush. If your two cards toward a Straight both happen to be Hearts, you'll have a Straight Flush for a clincher, but don't expect that very often.

Other sequences of three cards in a single suit offer the same hopes of a Straight or Flush, down to a hand such as ♠ : 5, 4, 3. But the higher brackets offer you better insurance if you happen to *pair up* a couple of your original cards. With ♥ : Q, J, 10, if you miss out on a Straight or Flush, but happen to get the Q ♦ and 10♠ as up cards, you will have a high Two Pair, which has a fair chance of winning, or perhaps get two Queens, Jacks or Tens, for Three of a Kind.

Starters like ♥ : A, K, Q are not as good, as they limit your chances for a Straight to a Ten and Nine. Starters like ♥ : K, Q, J are limited to an Ace and Ten or a Ten and Nine to make a Straight. Spaced starters, as ♥ : Q, 10, 8 or ♦ : 9, 7, 6 are also somewhat limited, but all are worth staying with.

Thus, if your fourth card fits with either your prospective Straight or Flush, stay right through to the finish, since you have three chances at filling on the fifth, sixth, or seventh. If you miss on the fourth card, stay for the fifth; if it hooks up with your original three, stay for the sixth and seventh, which will give you two chances for your Straight or Flush. But if you haven't improved by the fifth card, it's not worth the risk to stay any longer.

There is an exception to this. If you happen to make a high Pair on your fourth or fifth card, you can stay for the sixth or even the seventh, hoping to make a high Two Pair or Three of a Kind. This sometimes puts you back in the running toward a Straight or a Flush. For example:

Your Hand: **(K♥), (J♥), Q♥, 5♣, K♦, 9♥**

With ♥:K, Q, J for starters, you are dealt the useless **5♣**, but you stay, hoping for a fifth card that will help toward a Straight or Flush. When you are dealt the **K♦**, it just about ruins your hopes, but instead of folding, you stay on the chance of making Two Pair or Triplets since there are eleven cards that will do it (3 5s, 3 Js, 3 Qs and 2 Ks) and you have two more to come. Then, for your sixth card, up pops **9♥**, which gives you a dozen chances fill a Straight or a Flush on your seventh card.

In short, you wouldn't have stayed for that possible payoff, except for the prospects offered by the **K♥** which are still good. However, there are times when you would pass up such chances; and that's when other players have something better showing on the board, like Three of a Kind, four cards to a Flush, or Two Pair that could mean a Full House.

Three to a Flush: Here, with starters like ♠: K, 9, 4 you have up to a 20% chance of making a Flush, but some tight players would quit unless they were dealt another Spade as a fourth card. Usually, it's worth staying for a fifth card, particularly if the betting is light. Starters like ♦: J, 10, 5 are good, because you have three to a Flush and two to a Straight. If you miss a Diamond on your fourth card, but are dealt a Queen or a Nine, you will have three parts toward a Straight as well as three to a Flush, which make it worthwhile to go for a fifth card.

Three to a Straight: This can be handled like Three to a Flush. Nice, even if the suits are different, as **10♠, 9♥, 8♣;**

41

but nicer with two of the same suit, as **J♦, 10♥, 9♦**, as a Diamond for a fourth card will give you three parts to a Flush as well.

Pair in the Hole: A hand like **10♦, 10♥, Q♠** is good and even better if your up card gives you a start toward a Flush, as **9♦, 9♣, K♣**; or a Straight, as **Q♣, Q♥, J♥**. It's tough, though, if some other player has an up card of the same value as your hidden Pair, cutting your chance of Triplets in half. A hidden Pair is very nice to hold if you make a Full House, as many players will figure you for Three of a Kind and nothing more.

Split Pair, One Down — One Up: Some players fold on this, particularly with a low Pair, like **10♦, 4♣, 4♥**, as they think that staying on the visible **4♥** gives away the fact that they have another Four in the hole. However, a high Pair — say **6♣, K♦, K♥** — may convey the impression that you have a low Pair in the hole and are hoping to *pair up* the **K♥** to make Two Pair. If you do catch another King, you will have Triplets, which can fool the opposition very nicely. If your Split Pair also has two cards toward a Flush, or two toward a Straight, you will have that much more reason to stay.

Two to a Straight Flush, as **J♥, 10♥, 6♠** is a potential prospect and so is *Two to a Straight or Flush,* as **10♣, 9♦, 4♣**; but you will need immediate help from the fourth card and generally from the fifth as well. Two parts of a mere Flush — **3♦, 8♣, K♣** — or a mere Straight — **9♦, 8♠, A♥** — are apt to be useless; so is anything less.

A Sample Game

However, odd things can happen in a low-limit game where everybody stays. Here is an analysis of a typical deal:

	Louise	Kitty	Marvin	Nick	Oscar	Pauline
1st Card	(5♣)	(2♦)	(9♥)	(Q♠)	(2♠)	(8♥)
2nd Card	(5♠)	(7♥)	(K♠)	(8♦)	(6♦)	(Q♥)
3rd Card	3♣	7♣	3♠	4♥	5♦	10♥

Louise opens on a Pair of Fives, with two parts toward a Straight Flush — **5♣** and **3♣** — as a booster. Low, but good.

Kitty stays on a Pair of Sevens, one down, one up, but no boosters. Good enough in this game.

Marvin stays on two parts toward a Flush, represented by **K♠** as a hole card and **3♠** as up card.

Nick stays simply because his **Q♠** in the hole is higher than anything showing on the board. Definitely an unwise risk.

Oscar stays on two cards toward a Straight Flush — **5♦** and **6♦** — with the **2♠** as a hole card slightly helpful toward a Straight.

Pauline, with three parts of a Straight Flush — **♥ : Q, 10, 8** — considers raising, but holds off, waiting to see what the fourth card brings. This is good policy, since the starters are *spaced* where a Straight is concerned — Q, 10, 8 — and therefore fairly hard to fill.

Each player is dealt a fourth card, as follows:

	Louise	Kitty	Marvin	Nick	Oscar	Pauline
1st Card	(5♣)	(2♦)	(9♥)	(Q♠)	(2♠)	(8♥)
2nd Card	(5♠)	(7♥)	(K♠)	(8♦)	(6♦)	(Q♥)
3rd Card	3♣	7♣	3♠	4♥	5♦	10♥
4th Card	A♣	J♦	9♠	4♣	3♥	A♠

The fourth card is really the balance point in Seven Card Stud and represents a time to drop if the hand refuses to shape up. In this case, some interesting developments are seen.

Nick, with a Pair of Fours showing, simply checks to learn what happens. Though he's top man *on the board*, he realizes that he may not really belong in the game.

Oscar also checks, because the **3♥**, though helpful toward a Straight, will be useless unless he is dealt a Four; and Nick now has two of them.

Pauline checks with Ace-Ten, because her chance of filling a Straight is only slightly improved.

Louise, now with three parts toward a Club Flush and a hidden Pair of Fives, decides to bet and learn how strong Nick is.

Kitty, with a Pair of Sevens, naturally stays, as they beat anything on the board.

Marvin, who has hooked a Pair of Nines, stays for the same reason, noting that he now has three parts toward a Spade Flush.

Nick, Oscar and Pauline all decide to stay, as this is a low-limit game; and Nick, especially, would look foolish if he dropped after hooking a Pair of Fours.

The fifth and sixth cards, though bet separately, can be considered together, as nobody improved sufficiently to force the others out.

	Louise	Kitty	Marvin	Nick	Oscar	Pauline
1st Card	(5♣)	(2♦)	(9♥)	(Q♠)	(2♠)	(8♥)
2nd Card	(5♠)	(7♥)	(K♠)	(8♦)	(6♦)	(Q♥)
3rd Card	3♣	7♣	3♠	4♥	5♦	10♥
4th Card	A♣	J♦	9♠	4♣	3♥	A♠
5th Card	6♠	10♣	6♣	J♠	3♦	K♣
6th Card	K♥	A♥	J♣	9♣	2♥	A♦

After each player was dealt a fifth card, Nick was still high on the board with a Pair of Fours, with Oscar only a shade lower with a Pair of Threes. Both checked and so did the rest, for nobody actually held better than a Pair. All were hoping for something special on the sixth card and when Pauline came up with a Pair of Aces and promptly checked, the remaining players began to study the board quite closely.

Pauline's hand was almost an open book. She couldn't have Three Aces, because all four were showing on the board. Her chances of an Ace-high Straight were slight, because three Jacks were in view, all in other hands. With four up cards of different suits, she couldn't have a Flush. So Pauline's best was probably Two Pair, with a longshot chance of a Full House on the final card.

Louise also checked, hoping for Three Fives. Her up cards

showed that she couldn't have a Straight and if both her hole cards were Clubs, her chances for a Flush would be slight indeed with ten already in play, giving her only three chances out of 26 cards for another Club. (The 26 representing ten hole cards held by other players and 16 cards still in the pack).

Kitty looked good for Three Sevens, with only her 7♣ showing on the board, so when she also checked, everybody figured she was still after them. When Marvin checked, the players half-suspected that he had two Spades in the hole, as there were only five showing on the board, which made a Spade Flush a distinct possibility.

When Nick checked, it seemed obvious that he was after Three Fours and nothing else; but when Oscar suddenly bet, with only a Pair of Threes showing, the other players suddenly became excited. With four Diamonds showing on the board, Oscar could very well have two as hole cards, putting him in line for a Diamond Flush. Or he might have two Hearts in the hole, with only six showing on the board, giving him a chance for a Heart Flush. But since he couldn't be after both, all the other players decided to call him, each counting on improving his or her hand sufficiently to win.

Actually, Oscar was banking on the Two Pair that he already held; 3♦, 3♥, 2♠, 2♥. Small though it was, it might be a highest hand so far; and actually it was, since nobody else held Two Pair. But it wasn't all bluff on Oscar's part. He still had a chance for a Full House, for although he couldn't get a third Three, since all were showing on the board, there were two Deuces still unaccounted for and he might be dealt one of those for a 2-2-2-3-3 Full.

The seventh cards were dealt as down cards. Pauline checked; Louise bet; Kitty called; Marvin and Nick both folded. Oscar raised, Pauline folded; Louise and Kitty called. Here were the final cards they held:

	Louise	Kitty	Marvin	Nick	Oscar	Pauline
1st Card	(5♣)	(2♦)	(9♥)	(Q♠)	(2♠)	(8♥)
2nd Card	(5♠)	(7♥)	(K♠)	(8♦)	(6♦)	(Q♥)
3rd Card	3♣	7♣	3♠	4♥	5♦	10♥
4th Card	A♣	J♦	9♠	4♣	3♥	A♠
5th Card	6♠	10♣	6♣	J♠	3♦	K♣
6th Card	K♥	A♥	J♣	9♣	2♥	A♦
7th Card	(5♥)	(10♠)	(Q♦)	(6♥.)	(4♦)	(4♠)

Now to analyze the results:

Louise, like Oscar, was sharp enough to figure that the pot might be won with Two Pair. Apparently, Pauline didn't have Two Pair, or she would have bet them. That meant that if Louise caught either the K♠ or K♣ to go with her K♥, she would have the highest Two Pair. (K-K-5-5). Instead, she was dealt the *case* 5♥, on which she had dimly counted, giving her Three Fives, which looked like a real winner. Kitty, who was hot after Three Sevens, with two chances of making it, caught the 10♠ for Two Pair instead (10-10-7-7) but stayed, hoping it would stand up.

Note that Marvin and Nick were also after Two Pair and would have gotten them if their final cards had been transposed. That is, the 6♥ would have given Marvin 9-9-6-6; and the Q♦ would have given Nick Q-Q-4-4. That shows how close you can come to getting what you are after in Seven Card Stud and also how lucky you may be when you miss. For not only were Louise's Triplets better than any Two Pair, Oscar was a step higher.

Instead of catching one of those two Deuces for the 2-2-2-3-3 Full House that he wanted, Oscar was dealt the *case* 4♦, which he had almost forgotten as a prospect and it filled a nice low Straight 6-5-4-3-2 to take the pot. Surprises like that happen often in low-limit games of Seven Card Stud where everybody is inclined to stay on long chances.

In contrast, there are situations that arise in serious high-limit games which require more insight. Our next game covers just such a deal.

A Three Way Finish

There were six players in this game of Seven Card Stud — Alden, Brink, Cleary, Davis, Engle and Furlong. Taking it from Furlong's viewpoint, the first three cards dealt to each appeared thus:

Alden	*	*	5♣
Brink	*	*	10♠
Cleary	*	*	6♠
Davis	*	*	5♠
Engle	*	*	9♠
Furlong	(10♣)	(10♥)	J♥

Furlong opened with his Jack-high showing and was quite happy with a Pair of Tens in the hole and two parts toward a Straight Flush, the J♥ and 10♥. Alden folded his 5♣, Brink stayed with his 10♠. Cleary folded his 6♠, Davis did the same with the 5♠, but Engle stayed with his 9♠.

With each succeeding round, Furlong still was high and bet first in each case, with Brink and Engle staying as they had before, until the sixth card had been dealt. The board then stood as shown below, still from Furlong's viewpoint:

Brink	*	*	10♠	A♣	10♦	K♥
Engle	*	*	9♠	7♦	8♣	7♣
Furlong	(10♣)	(10♥)	J♥	A♥	A♦	6♥

After Furlong bet and others stayed, Furlong sized up the situation thus: Brink was probably going for an Ace-high Straight, with no chance whatever of a Flush, because Brink's four up cards were of different suits. If Brink has the A♠ as a hole card, he couldn't get anything higher than Two Pair — Aces over Tens — because Furlong had two tens as hole cards and a Pair of Aces as up cards. Thus Furlong was in an ideal situation to judge Brink's limitations.

The same applied to Engle. With a 9-8-7 on display, he appeared to be going for a Straight, too. Only it couldn't be a 10-high, because Brink showed two Tens and Furlong had two in the hole. So it would have to be 9-8-7-6-5, which was highly unlikely, as a wise player like Engle would hardly stay with such low hole cards. Thus Brink could size Engle for a 10-high Straight, because Brink didn't know that Furlong held the only available Tens. But Furlong recognized Engle's limitation, which had a lot to do with what followed.

Each was dealt a seventh card, face down. Furlong checked and Brink bet the limit. Engle, ignoring Brink's possible Ace-high, raised with his apparent 10-high Straight. But Furlong saw it differently. A 10-high Straight was out for Engle; and so, most probably, was a 9-high, because Furlong remembered Alden had turned down the 5♣, Cleary the 6♠, and Davis the 5♠. Also, Furlong's own sixth card, the 6♥, lessened Engle's chances still more.

And for a final clincher, Furlong was dealt the 5♥ as his seventh card, a down card, so his hand finally stood:

Furlong   (10♣) (10♥)   J♥   A♥   A♦   6♥
    (5♥)

That really reduced Engle's chance of a 9-high Straight. More importantly, it gave Furlong the very hand he was after, a Heart Flush headed by the Ace — running A♥, J♥, 10♥, 6♥, 5♥. So if Engle hadn't raised, Furlong would have, for his hand looked like a sure winner.

But now, instead of raising, Furlong didn't even call the bet. Instead, he folded his Ace-high Flush and dropped out! Furlong's reasoning was:

Brink must have his A-K-Q-J-10, or he wouldn't have bet so steadily, unless he was trying to bluff Engle, who in turn might suppose that Brink was bluffing. Remember, however, that Brink could well believe that Engle held either a 10-9-8-7-6 or a 9-8-7-6-5, while Furlong knew that a 10-high was out and a 9-high probably so. Furlong was sure that Engle must have something strong enough to beat any Straight, otherwise, he would simply have called Brink's bluff, instead of raising him.

Possibly Engle held a Club Flush. If one of his original hole cards happened to be the **9♣**, and the other a high Club, such as the **K♣**, his fifth and sixth cards – **8♣** and **7♣** — would give him a Four Flush and another Club as his final down card would complete the Flush. But that raised another prospect. Both Brink and Engle knew that Furlong could be after a Heart Flush, with three Hearts as up cards; and that he had a good chance of making it, with so few other Hearts in evidence. Of course, they could be betting that Furlong hadn't made his Flush; but if so, Engle should have left it up to Furlong to raise.

If Engle felt that he had Brink's Ace-high Straight beaten, thanks to his Flush, he would want to be equally sure that he had Furlong's possible Flush beaten. But Engle's Club Flush could only be King-high, since the **A♣** was showing in Brink's hand; whereas Furlong's Heart Flush was obviously Ace-high. What was more, Furlong doubted that Engle had been going for a Club Flush, since the two essential cards (**8♣** and **7♣**) hadn't shown until late. So Furlong decided that Engle had something bigger than a Flush; and that was why Furlong folded.

Brink didn't give up that easily — or that wisely. He called Engle's raise and the showdown proved that Furlong was right. Here were the hands:

Brink	(Q♠)	(J♠)	10♠	A♣	10♦	K♥	(4♦)
Engle	(8♦)	(9♦)	9♠	7♦	8♣	7♣	(8♠)

Engle hadn't been counting on either a Straight or Flush after his fifth card (**8♣**) turned up. He then began thinking in terms of a Full House (9-9-9-8-8 or 8-8-8-9-9-). When the **7♣** popped up as the sixth card, he found himself stuck with "Three Pair" (9-9, 8-8, 7-7) which is practically worthless in Seven Card Stud. But he still had another card to come and his hit of the **8♠** gave him the Full House he wanted, just as Furlong wanted that last Heart, which he could have done without.

So the winner was Engle, with his Full House.
Engle: **8♦, 8♣, 8♠, 9♦, 9♠** (or **7♦, 7♣**)

The runner-up was Furlong, with his Flush:
Furlong: **A♥, J♥, 10♥, 6♥, 5♥**

And the lower was Brink with his Straight:
Brink: **A♣, K♥, Q♠, J♠, 10♠**

The real winner, in the long run, was Furlong. He saved enough by dropping to bet the limit in a future hand where he had practically a sure thing. Moreover, since he folded, he did not have to show his hand, so none of the other players knew whether he had his Heart Flush, or was merely aiming for it and dropped because he didn't make it.

Eight Card Stud

Just like Seven Card Stud, but an eighth card is dealt face down and there is an additional betting round. With four down cards, it is much more difficult to guess the contents of another player's hand. More care must be taken in declaring hands, as more combinations are possible.

Since each player is able to reject three odd cards instead of only two, the hands hit a higher average than in Seven Card Stud, but the game is still sufficiently controlled to be regarded as sound Poker.

There are two options with Eight Card Stud.

1. Deal the 7th card face up and the 8th face down, or vice versa.

2. Deal the 7th and 8th cards together, so both are bet on the same round.

Nine and Ten Card Stud

These call for additional cards, resulting in hands that are too freakish for regular Poker play. The number of down cards and how they should be dealt for betting rounds should be decided upon beforehand.

In all forms of stud, if cards run short because of too many players, cards from folded hands are shuffled and used.

Flip Stud

Originally termed Mexican Stud or Pedro, this is simply Five Card Stud, with the first two cards dealt face down, giving the player the privilege of keeping either for his hole card and turning up the other. With time, this was extended to allow the same choice with each succeeding card being dealt face down, so the player could keep it face down and then *flip* his hole card face up.

Thus the game became known as Flip and eventually other innovations were added. With Deuces Wild, a player naturally keeps a Deuce as downcard, unless he wants to bluff people into thinking he has two. The same applies to any other wild cards that may be named in Dealer's Choice. Another game is played with each player's first up card wild for his hand, along with others of that value. This is sometimes termed Shifting Sands. It is also played with each player's hole card wild, under the name of Rickey de Laet. This is wilder, but allows smarter play.

Other forms of Stud can be played as Flip, most notably Seven Card Flip. In this, three cards were originally dealt face down, letting the player flip the one he wants as up card. From then on it can be regular Seven Card Stud, or the flip privilege can be extended. Another popular form is to deal four cards face down, with the player turning up two to start the first betting round; after that, no flips are allowed.

All forms of Flip can be played as High-Low Poker.

IV

SIMPLE
VARIATIONS
OF POKER

Under this head are forms of Poker which follow the pattern of the standard game, with added touches that speed the action, but do not turn it into a wild game. Some groups play these regularly, while others introduce them as a form of Dealer's Choice. Perhaps the oldest and most popular is:

Draw Poker with the Stripped Pack Here, with five players or less, the lower values are removed from the pack, reducing it to 44 cards (without Deuces or Threes), 40 cards (without Fours as well) or even less by removing Fives, and even Sixes. When Aces are regarded as low they rank just below the lowest value still remaining in the pack. For example, with a 32-card pack, running down to Sevens, the lowest Straight would be 10,9,8,7,A.

This means that the chances of receiving or improving high hands in a three, four or five player game are increased to those of a six, seven, or eight-handed game, or sometimes greater, according to the number of cards removed from the pack. The idea is to strike a balance that will enliven the game without spoiling it.

Four Flush as Opener This is Jackpots, except that a player can open with a Four Flush (four cards of one suit) as well as a Pair of Jacks or better. This encourages a player to go after a one-card draw in hopes of making a Flush. Similarly:

Bobtail as Opener Allows a player to open on a Bobtail Straight (four cards in sequence, as Q,J,10,9) as well as a Four Flush, which also can profit from a one-card draw.

Acepots is a term applied to a game where a Pair of Aces or better is required, making it a stepped-up form of Jackpots.

Simple Variations in Five Card Stud include games in which a Four Flush is either rated just below a Pair, or just above a Pair. In the latter form, it is popularly termed New York Stud. Sometimes, in such games, a Bobtail, or Four-card Straight is rated just below a Four Flush. It is then known as Canada Stud. In both forms, players naturally stay with such hands, though ordinarily they might drop early.

Hole Card Stud is the regular Five Card game, but the first card is dealt singly, as a face-down hole card and there is a round of betting before the second card is dealt as an up card. This game is sometimes called Pistol or Pistol Pete, though some people apply those terms only when the game is played High-Low. Another innovation is to deal the fifth card face down as a second hole card. This is sometimes called Five Card Final.

In some games, a player is dealt an extra card as an option to replace one of his five, either down or up, as it may happen to be. This game naturally came to be called Option, though it is also known as English Stud, a term which generally signifies that the game is to be played High-Low.

Don't confuse this with *Seven Card Stud — English Style,* which is played like Seven Card Stud, but with two optional replacements at the finish, each with a betting round, so a player can actually have the choice of nine cards to make up his five-card hand.

V

DEALER'S CHOICE

The term Dealer's Choice applies to Poker games in which the dealer can name the type of game to be played during that hand. This may be limited to those already described and in some cases, a few of those — Eight or Nine Card Stud — may be disallowed. But in many social circles where the play is for small limits, Dealer's Choice may include a great variety of *wild* games, often with no restrictions whatever. Some of these are far removed from standard Poker, but many people regard them as fun. These games include the following.

Joker Wild

Joker Wild is the most reserved of wild games, in which a Joker is simply added to the pack and may represent any card that the holder names. Thus the highest hand becomes Five of a Kind, as a player holding Four Aces can call the Joker a fifth Ace of any suit. This takes precedence over a Royal Flush.

As part of an Ace-high Flush, a Joker can also represent a duplicate Ace, making his hand higher than a rival Ace-high Flush. Most often, the Joker is used to fill a hand like a Full House, or a Straight. The Joker, with a Pair, makes Three of a Kind; with Three of a Kind, it gives the player Four of a Kind.

Sometimes the use of the Joker is restricted to Ace, Straights or Flushes, but the modern trend is to make it completely wild.

Two Jokers may be included in the pack, making the game Double Joker Wild.

Deuces Wild

Deuces Wild is played with the regular 52-card pack, the Deuces become wild, representing any card of any suit. In this game, Five of a Kind is the highest hand, followed by a Royal Flush and so on down. In case of *ties,* it may be agreed that a *natural* hand takes precedence, so that a Straight consisting of J ♥, 10♠, 9 ♥, 8♠, 7 ♥ would beat out one composed of J ♦, 2♠, 9♣, 8♣, 7♠. However, with a game being wild any embellishments may be added.

One question that should be decided at the outset is this: Should a Deuce be allowed to represent a card already in a player's hand, as in Joker Wild? Generally, players will agree that it should, so if that rule is included, it becomes possible for a player to hold a Double Ace Flush. For example: 2♣, 2♥, 10 ♦, 5 ♦, 3 ♦ would be regarded as a Diamond Flush, which would run: A ♦, A ♦, 10 ♦, 5 ♦, 3 ♥.

Thanks to the Double Ace such a Flush would beat a Flush such as A♣, K♣, J♣, 9♣, 8♣, which has only a single Ace, even though its next best card is a King.

In Deuces Wild, the highest combination is Five of a Kind and a player holding all four Deuces has an invincible hand, because nobody else can make Five of a Kind. In his case, Five Threes are just as good as Five Aces.

With three Deuces, or less, a player can still make Five of a Kind, but he will need Five Aces to be invincible. Here are the possible combinations:

2♥,	2♦,	2♣,	A♠,	A♣	=	A-A-A-A-A
2♥,	2♦,	A♠,	A♣,	A♥,	=	A-A-A-A-A
2♥,	A♠,	A♣,	A♥,	A♦	=	A-A-A-A-A

This shows that Deuces have a double value, since the more

of them a player holds, the stronger his hand can become, while opposing hands are apt to be all the weaker, due to their lack of Deuces. If you hold three Deucés, you automatically will have Four of a Kind, which is pretty tough for anyone else to beat with only one Deuce at his disposal.

This brings up another important factor in Deuces Wild; unlike standard Poker, the cards do *not* speak for themselves when you lay down a five-card hand including one Deuce or more. For example: **2♥, 2♦, A♥, 6♠, 6♣**

A player with such a hand might have his mind so fixed on Aces that he would announce his hand as an "Ace-High Full" — A,A,A,6,6, overlooking his chance to class each Deuce as a Six, thus giving him Four Sixes. That would be a costly oversight if some rival player happened to hold Four Fives!

As another case: **2♣, 2♦, 2♠, Q♣, 8♣**

Here, by classing each Deuce as a Queen, a player would make Four Queens, a strong hand indeed, yet one that he could improve by considering the three Deuces as **J♣, 10♣, 9♣,** giving him a Queen High Straight Flush, running **♣: Q, J, 10, 9, 8.** He would need it, too, if another player happened to be holding three Kings with the odd Deuce, which would stand for Four Kings.

These are a few preliminaries which must be kept constantly in mind when delving into the various forms of Deuces Wild that follow.

Draw Poker With Deuces Wild

Even though there are wild cards in this game, the game itself is far from being wild. In a five or six hand game, you can often calculate your chances just as keenly as you would in standard Draw Poker, but the comparative values of different combinations are changed and the questions of when to draw and what to draw take on new aspects.

In regular Draw, if most of the players stay, a high Two Pair (as K,K,9,9) may be an average winner. With Deuces Wild, Three Aces rate in that capacity. But the player who uses that as his yardstick is apt to come a cropper, for the simple reason that there are *three ways* to hold Three Aces:

A-A-A   2-A-A   2-2-A

Suppose there are six players in the game; the betting has been low and five have stayed, drawing two or three cards each. You stayed with two Aces and caught a third, but nothing more. So you have what you think should be an average winner; but not in this case! The reason being there were 30 cards dealt to start and 12 drawn, total of 42. Chances are that *three* of the Deuces, and maybe the *fourth,* are in the rival hands. What if one filled a Three-Flush? What if a player held a Pair of Deuces and drew a Pair of Sevens to make Four of a Kind? Where would your Three Aces be? Answer: In the discard, where you might do better to toss them instead of betting them.

However, if you are holding Deuce-Ace-Ace as Three Aces, there is one less Deuce out against you; and if you hold Deuce-Deuce-Ace, nobody can have more Deuces than you. This covers the situation *after* the draw, when the hands are finally shown. But Deuces — or the lack of them — can have an important bearing on the draw itself. So here are some guidelines to be considered *before* the draw.

Don't stay on a *natural* Pair — even as high as Aces — if most of the other players stay, as that means most of the Deuces may be out against you, lessening any chance of improving your hand. However, if only one or two players stay, you can afford to do the same in a low-limit game, as you may catch a Deuce to go along with your Pair.

Two Pair are a snare and a delusion. They have to be *naturals,* as a Deuce would turn any Pair into Triplets. If you draw one card to Two Pair, your normal chance of getting a

Full House is 4 out of 47, or only about one chance in twelve. With Deuces Wild, this becomes 8 out of 47, or one chance in six, but that is still not good enough; again, if most of the other players stay, they will probably have the Deuces that you need so badly. So it's smart to drop with Two Pair.

Staying on a *natural* Three of a Kind is generally good policy. Instead of having to depend on one lone card out of 47 to make Four of a Kind, there are five that will do it; the lone card plus the four Deuces. Also, there are chances of making a Full House. If practically everybody else stays, you might do well to drop, particularly if somebody bumps the pot, as they're not likely to *bump the pot* without a Deuce in hand.

Four parts toward a *natural* Straight gives staying qualities to your hand. Here, an Inside Straight — as Q,J,*,9,8 — is as good as an *open-ender* like Q,J,10,9 in standard Draw Poker, because you have eight chances to fill, as there are four Tens and four Deuces that will complete your Q,J,10,9,8 or Q,J,2,9,8. With a Bobtail, as an *open-ender* is also called, your chances are increased to 12 out of 47, or about one in four in Deuces Wild, which is quite worthwhile.

A *natural* Four Flush also provides a good chance for a *fill*, 13 out of 47 to be exact, which is better than one in four. But with either a Straight or Flush, it is better to fill with a Deuce than some other card, because that means one less Deuce out against you, thus giving your Straight or Flush a better chance of standing up.

Of course a player should stay on a *pat* Straight or Flush, as well as a *natural* Full House. With a *natural* Four of a Kind, he should always draw one card in hope of catching a Deuce for Five of a Kind. Four parts toward a *natural* Straight Flush offer as many as 18 out of 47 chances for a *fill*; and if one is dealt to you *pat*, it is a very healthy holding, usually worth a limit bet.

Where Deuces are dealt to a player before the draw, there are special factors to be considered. In most games, the average player will stay on the strength of a single Deuce, though he should really have a high card to go with it, thus giving him a high Pair to start. But even there, some moot points can arise. For example: **2♦, K♠, 7♥, 6♣, 5♥**.

Here, a player has the equivalent of a Pair of Kings (2-K) so he could logically discard the other cards and draw three to replace them. But if he discards the King and draws a single card, he can make a Straight by drawing a Nine, an Eight, a Four, a Three, or a Deuce — a total of 19 cards out of 47, which is pretty close to an even chance.

With a Pair and a Deuce, a player automatically has Three of a Kind and should draw two in hopes of making a Full House or Four of a Kind. The exception to this rule is when he also has four parts toward a Straight Flush, which becomes a better draw. For example: **2♥, Q♣, Q♦, J♦, 10♦**.

Holding 2-Q-Q, there are five cards that will make Four Queens; namely, three Deuces and two Queens, with two chances of drawing one. But holding **2♥, Q♦, J♦, 10♦** brings seven chances for a Straight Flush, consisting of three Deuces or the Ace, King, Nine, Eight of Diamonds. The player can only draw one card in this case, but he also has 12 chances of filling a Straight and five of filling a Flush.

With a Pair of Deuces in your hand, it is often best to discard the others and draw to the Deuces alone, unless you have a *pat* hand to start. With Three Deuces in hand, you are sure of Four of a Kind, no matter what you draw, but of course you would do well to stand pat if you are already holding a Straight Flush.

Various Wild Card Games

Any form of Stud Poker can be played with Deuces Wild, if the dealer so chooses. With Five Card Stud, the game is apt to be erratic, as the appearance of a Deuce as an up card may cause all the other players to fold. Six Card Stud is better and Seven Card Stud is best with Deuces Wild, because it gives players just enough leeway to improve their hands without prolonging the agony, as may occur with Eight, Nine, or Ten Card Stud with Deuces Wild.

Hence Seven Card Stud Deuces Wild, will be stressed in the section that follows, along with two offshoots, Low Hole Card Wild and Baseball, which can also be played as Five Card Stud. Other variants may be improvised by players to suit themselves, as there is no limit to the trend that wild games can take.

This brings up another phase, namely, that the wild cards themselves are not always limited to Deuces. Some popular forms include:

One-Eyed Jacks Wild There are two of these cards, the Jack of Hearts and Jack of Spades, called ''one-eyed'' because they are depicted in profile.

Mustached Kings Wild There are three of these, the King of Diamonds, King of Spades and King of Clubs.

Deuces and Treys Wild Here, Treys (Threes) are considered wild along with Deuces, making eight wild cards in all.

One Card Wild Each player calls one of his cards wild. In Draw, he might show a Pair of Eights with a Pair of Threes and a Jack, calling the latter *wild* for a Full House, 8,8,8,3,3.

One Value Wild With the same Pair of Eights, Pair of Threes and an odd Jack, the player would specify Threes as his *wild value,* making them both wild, which would give him 8,8,8,8,J for Four Eights.

One Suit Wild All cards of a specified suit named by the dealer (before the deal) are declared wild. If the dealer should name *Spades* a hand consisting of 5♠, 4♠, 10♥, 9♥, 6♥, would be a Straight Flush in Hearts, ♥, 10, 9, 8, 7, 6.

All Pictures Wild In this variant all picture cards, Kings, Queens and Jacks are regarded as wild in all hands.

Name Your Poison Before the deal, the player names cards of any value he wants to be wild in all hands; as Aces, Jacks, Fives, etc., including two or more values if he prefers.

Seven Card Stud — Deuces Wild

Adding *wild* Deuces to Seven Card Stud gives a keen player a decided edge, just as with Draw Poker. The gimmick is the same; you go for the deuces and try to figure who else is doing the same. There are however, other factors which give the game a different twist. Accordingly, a player may find it profitable to switch from Draw with Deuces to Seven Card with Deuces and sometimes vice versa, when he has Dealer's Choice.

By way of contrast, consider a seven-handed game. In Draw, each player gets five cards face down (a total of 35), so in many cases, three of the deuces are immediately dealt. This discourages any players who fail to receive a deuce, and they are apt to drop so fast that the game becomes unbearably tight. The chance of somebody being dealt two deuces also scares conservative players, particularly after they've lost a few pots against such hands.

In the same seven-handed session, only two cards are dealt face down at the start when playing Seven Card Stud. That makes 14 in all, so with Deuces Wild, the law of averages indicates that only one player will have a deuce as a hole card. The result being that players often stay for a card or two on almost anything, hoping a Deuce will *put them in the chips*.

Note: In this game, as with other forms of Stud with Deuces Wild, the betting is opened by the first player to the dealer's left who shows a Deuce as up card. If no Deuces show, the highest up card opens, as in standard Stud. After the first betting round, the player with the highest combination bets. Thus, with two up cards showing, A-A, 2-A, or 2-2 would each represent a Pair of Aces and the first player holding one of those would bet. Otherwise, it would range downward from a Pair of Kings.

Some stay on starters that they would pass up in standard Seven Card Stud. A player named Barney was a good example. In the regular game, he followed the rule of staying only on three parts to a Straight or Flush, a high Pair, or a low *hole* Pair with a high up card. But with Deuces Wild, he would go on a small Pair, down and up — as (6 ♦) (8 ♥) 6 ♣ — unless a Deuce was showing on the board; he wouldn't be happy unless he had one himself. He also regarded a setup like (5 ♥) (7 ♥) 5 ♣ as a powerful prospect because a Deuce would produce Three Fives or three parts to a Straight Flush. In one six-player game of Seven Card Deuces Wild, Barney loosened so much that he let his hopes run away with him. By the fifth card, three players had folded and when the sixth card was dealt, there were just three left: A keen player named Garry, our friend Barney and another man, Whitey.

Their hands looked like this:

Garry	*	*	2♣	J♠	10♥	Q♦
Barney	*	*	7♦	5♣	A♣	K♣
Whitey	*	*	K♦	5♦	10♣	8♣
4th Man	*	*	6♥	(Folded)		
5th Man	*	*	10♠	3♥	(Folded)	
6th Man	*	*	4♣	(Folded)		

Garry made a sizable bet and immediately the others pegged him for a Straight even though two kings were showing on the board. There were two Kings still at large and four Nines absent, with three Aces and three Eights still unheard from. With any one of those twelve cards in the hole, Garry could have a Straight A, K, Q, J, 10, or K, Q, J, 10, 9, or even Q, J, 10, 9, — — with the 2♣ serving for one of those values.

Since Barney recognized that, why did Barney raise?

Garry had the answer to that. Since Garry had a Deuce as his original up card, he was sure that Barney must have one in the hole although that wasn't enough to justify a raise on Barney's part, who was the type who didn't bet them unless he had them. So Garry figured that Barney also had a Seven in the hole, giving him Three of a Kind from the start; but Triplets weren't enough for Barney to raise Garry's bet when Garry had a Straight already clinched.

So Garry decided that Barney's Seven in the hole must be the Seven of Clubs. Barney had strung along on the strength of Three Sevens — one a Deuce — and when three Clubs in a row had popped up, he found himself sitting with a Club Flush — A♣, K♣, Deuce (for Q♣), 7♣ and 5♣. Since Barney's Flush was higher than Garry's Straight, Barney naturally raised.

While Garry was rationalizing all that, Whitey folded. Apparently, he had been counting on a Diamond Flush — with his K♦ and 5♦ — only to have a couple of Clubs show up. Even if he did have two Diamonds in the hole, it wouldn't help if he picked up another as a seventh card, because Barney already had a Club Flush headed by an Ace-King, which would have beaten Whitey's King-high Diamond Flush.

That's the way you think ahead in Seven Card Stud with Deuces Wild, which is why so many people like the game. Anyway, after Whitey folded, Garry called Barney's raise. It could be that Garry thought Barney was bluffing and didn't really have a Flush, which was unlikely, as Barney had never been known to bluff. Barney decided that Garry must have a Pair of Nines in the hole and was hoping he could gain a Queen, Jack or Ten as a seventh card to fill a Full House, which would beat Barney's Flush, But Barney, too, had prospects.

Thus, when the seventh card was dealt, face down, it was up to Garry to bet again, since on the board he was still *high man* with his Pair of Queens — Q♦ and 2♣ — so he bet the limit. Barney raised the limit, to see if Garry had made it. Garry raised the limit, which meant that he had made it, too. Barney then called, not just through charity, but because he liked to pick up his winnings as fast as possible.

Only, this time, Barney didn't pick them up. When the hole cards were turned up, they showed these hands:

Garry: (Q♥) (J♥)   2♣   J♠   10♥   Q♦   (Q♠)
Barney: (7♣) (2♥)   7♦   5♣   A♣   K♣   (A♦)

So Garry was the winner, with Four Queens — Q♥, 2♣, Q♦, Q♠ — over Barney's Full House: 2♥, A♣, A♦, 7♣, 7♦.

Needless to say, Barney was shocked at the outcome and insisted that if they had had a showdown on the sixth card, his Flush would have taken Garry's Straight.

Garry just smiled and said nothing. He didn't point out that Barney had read the cards wrong all along. Study them yourself and you will see why. Garry didn't have the sure-fire Straight that Barney was so sure he held, because four parts of it — 2♣, J♠, 10♥, Q♦ — were showing as up cards. What he did have, thanks to his hole cards, was a Full House: Q♥, 2♣, Q♦, J♥, J♠, which was better than the Club Flush that Barney apparently had.

So Garry bet his apparent Straight to see if Barney would raise on his actual Flush, which Barney did. Then Garry called as if Barney's real Flush had beaten his imaginary Straight. Garry knew that his Full House was actually the top hand. But now, Garry was calculating the odds that still lay ahead, if both Barney and he should connect on the seventh cards, as they might.

Before the seventh card was dealt, there were 32 unknown cards from Garry's viewpoint. He knew his two hole cards and felt sure of Barney's two hole cards. Those four, plus 16 up cards, totaled 20 *known* cards, which substracted from the full pack of 52, left 32 *unknowns*. Of those 32 cards, Barney had three chances — A♦, A♠, A♥ — of making an Ace-high Full House, which would beat Garry's existing Queen-high Full. In addition to four chances (2♦, 2♠, 7♥, 7♠) of making Four Sevens, which would do the same, a total of seven chances in all.

In contrast, Garry had four chances — 2♦, 2♠, A♥, K♥

— toward a Royal Flush in Hearts; two chances — **9 ♥** and **8 ♥** — toward a Straight Flush; and four chances — **Q ♠, Q ♣, J ♦, J ♣** — toward Four of a Kind that would be higher than Barney's Four Sevens. That totaled ten chances in all that if Barney bettered Garry, Garry would better Barney, which he did. So Garry's "luck" was simply that Barney was so busy calculating his own chances that he didn't think about Garry's. When Seven Card Stud goes wild, some players go wild with it; not necessarily in their play, but in the way they figure the odds.

Here is Garry's own general summary of Seven Card Stud with Deuces Wild:

Straights are shaky and not worth going after, even with your first three cards in sequence, as **10 ♠, 9 ♥, 8 ♣,** unless two are of the same suit, as **10 ♣, 9 ♦, 8 ♦**. If you fall into a Straight, it can only win when other players fail to improve Two Pair of Three of a Kind, thus coming up with a Full House or Four of a Kind.

A high Flush is often a good bet, particularly against players who go for Straights and Flushes. But in a steep game, you need a Full House or better. This makes sense, because in standard Seven Card Stud, Two Pair or Three of a Kind are frequent winners, so add a Deuce to each and you have a Full House or Four of a Kind.

Low Hole Card Wild

This is a great game for those who are disappointed with Deuces Wild, because it guarantees each player one wild card — or more — in every hand. His lowest card, of the first, second or seventh dealt him, counts as low for his individual hand, as do any other cards of that same value which are dealt to him. Just what his wild card is, nobody else knows until he reveals his hole cards. Then, the reckoning begins.

It is nice to have someone call for this game in Dealer's Choice, because many players figure it wrong and ride along on hands that they should throw away. That adds extra dividends to ordinary pots, even though the betting may not be very heavy. They go on the assumption that since a Full House is an average winner in Deuces Wild, the same should hold in Low Hole Card Wild.

It does apply, but only when three or four players are all dealt the same low hole card and everybody else drops. In the majority of hands, as many as three or four players may each have a special wild card, which beefs up the game to the point where a high Four of a Kind or even a Straight Flush should be rated as an average win.

There are times, however, when a player's monopoly of a certain hole card, say a Five as his low, may be marred when cards of that same value appear as up cards in opposing hands. Also, a nice *low* holding of wild cards can be ruined by the final hole card. Here was just such a heart-breaker, in a game that narrowed down to two Players.

| Bob | (3♣) | (K♠) | 3♦ | 7♠ | K♣ | 3♥ |
| Ray | * | * | J♥ | 10♦ | 4♠ | A♠ |

Bob, with a Three as his wild card, had an almost unbeatable Five Kings — 3,3,3,K,K — until his final hold card. Then:

| Bob | (3♣) | (K♠) | 3♦ | 7♠ | K♣ | 3♥ | (2♣) |
| Ray | (10♥) | (4♣) | J♥ | 10♦ | 4♠ | A♠ | (6♥) |

The Deuce became Bob's wild card, reducing his hand to a mere Four Threes (2,3,3,3) which Ray topped with Four Tens (4,4,10,10).

Some players fold on fairly high hole cards, rather than get undercut on the final; but that can work in reverse. Here was a case in point:

| Alf | (6♣) | (9♥) | 8♣ | 9♣ | 10♣ | Q♠ |
| Bob | * | * | J♥ | J♣ | 6♠ | 6♥ |

66

Cal	*	*	Q♥	10♦	10♠	Q♣
Doc	*	*	7♦	6♦	7♣	3♦
Ed	*	*	5♣	8♥	(Folded)	

Alf was after a straight Flush in Clubs. To fill it, he needed the **Q♣**, **J♣**, **7♣**, or a *wild* **6♠**, **6♥**, **6♦**. However, all such possible ''fills'' were up cards in other hands. Still, Alf stayed when bets were made on the sixth card. Why? Because there were 3 Fives, 4 Fours, 3 Threes, and 4 Deuces still at large. Any one of those would automatically become Alf's wild card, giving him ♣ **10,9,8,7,6,** with the wild card as the **7♣** and the **6♣** as itself.

As it happened, Alf was dealt the **4♠**, which wasn't surprising as he had 14 out of 32 chances of catching a *new* wild card. That shows how it pays to *stay* in Low Hole Card Wild. The question is how long you should stay? A good rule is to fold on the fifth card unless it gives you a high Three of a Kind or four parts of a Straight Flush.

From there on, you are on your own. By studying the other up cards, you can figure your chances on Four of a Kind, a Straight Flush, or better still, Five of a Kind. One good thing about this game; you don't have to give away your hand when you bet. Your wild card is your own secret until the showdown.

VI

BASEBALL

Some experts regard this game as *highly wild,* but actually Baseball has well-defined limitations, which render it quite keen. The basic game, which is still the best, has rules that are easy to remember because they are based on the game of Baseball. This blending of America's two national games — Poker and Baseball — operates as follows:

Players are dealt three cards each, two face down, as hole cards, and one face up. A round of betting follows, and players are dealt three more up cards, each followed by a betting round, and finally a down card, with another betting round. That makes it very much like Seven Card Stud, or more properly, Seven Card Stud, Deuces Wild, for there are wild cards in this game, too. But therein lies the difference, because:

All Nines are wild, which is easily remembered, because there are nine players on a baseball team and nine innings in a game. Threes are wild, too, because there are three outs in an inning. But here comes the special angle that adds punch to the game.

A Three is wild when dealt as a hole card only. If it is dealt as an up card, it can mean Three strikes and Out where the player is concerned, unless he is willing to pay a special penalty. He must match the amount of the pot. If he does, he is entitled to keep his Three as a wild up card.

When this happens, it is really great Poker, because the element of bluff is strong. If a player is willing to match the pot, it would seem that he had very strong hole cards and needed another wild one as a clincher. But Poker is a game of bluff — remember? — so to pay a nice price for an *up three* is apt to make other players think that you have something that you don't have. That's good Poker!

Even better is this: If you are dealt a Four as an up card, you have a special privilege. In real baseball, a player who is served four balls is entitled to a free trip to first base. So in this game, a player who is dealt a four as an up card, is given the same privilege. He is promptly dealt a free card, as a down card giving him an extra in his hand, which may — or may not — prove to be an important adjunct.

Actually, Baseball is not as wild a game as many people suppose. It's about the same as any Seven Card Stud game in which two values are specified as wild, say Deuces and Sevens. In Baseball, it's Threes and Nines wild, instead. The fact that a Four as up card gives a player a free down card is offset by the fact that another player is apt to fold if dealt a Three. These are factors that pep up the game and give it a strong individuality.

It isn't difficult to recognize tight players in Baseball. They're afraid of those costly Threes and are irked whenever an opponent gets a free card for a Four. In a game of Dealer's Choice, they seldom, if ever, call for Baseball as their own choice. So a tight player is not apt to open or stay after the first three cards are dealt for the opening betting round, unless he is dealt one of the following combinations:

Three Wild Cards, two down, one up.
   (9♥) (9♠) 3♦
Two Wild Cards, both in the hole.
   (9♣) (3♣) 6♥

Two Wild Cards, one down, one up.

(9 ♦) (7 ♣) 3 ♥

A Wild Card and a Pair above Eights.

(K ♥) (K ♠) 3 ♠

A Wild Card and two parts to a Royal Flush.

(3 ♠) (K ♦) 10 ♦

A Natural Three of a Kind above Eights.

(Q ♦) (Q ♥) Q ♣

At this early stage, if a tight player is dealt a Three as his up card, he must match the pot as soon as the card is dealt and since nobody has had a chance to bet, the pot will contain nothing more than the ante, so it's cheap enough to stay with a Three if a player's cards come up to opening requirements. If a Four is dealt as a player's up card, he is given a down card immediately, so he is able to peek and see if it improves his hand. Some tight players will sometimes *stay* even if the extra is below par, for there is a certain advantage in having three hole cards at the start and an eighth card at the finish.

Smart players will frequently stay on less than tight requirements for several good reasons. First, hands that start off well often fade out badly. Second, a fairly good hand may show surprising improvement as the deal proceeds. Finally, and most importantly, it is quite possible to *read* a tight player's hand almost to exactitude, thereby recognizing when you have him beaten. If you aren't sure about a player, consider him to be *tight*. Usually, he will be working on less than a tight player would demand, so he is apt to fall by the wayside.

Some students of Baseball Poker class Four Eights as the minimum for a winning hand, so it is smart to set your sights on something higher, right from the start. In keeping with that estimate, there is a record of a six-player game in which five players stayed through one deal and wound up in the following order:

1) Four Kings (K-K-K-3)

2) Four Queens (Q-Q-Q-3)
3) Four Jacks (J-9-9-9)
4) Four Tens (10-10-10-3)
5) Four Eights (8-8-8-3)

All above minimum, but none much above. Oddly, the third man had two Wild Nines and caught another quite soon, but couldn't pair up any of the rest or catch two of the same suit that were close enough for a Straight Flush. The fifth man was dealt two Fours as up cards, giving him two extras in the hole, but he still couldn't do better than Four Eights.

The big menace in this game is Five of a Kind. Theoretically, such hands should show up more often than they do, because tight players are apt to fold too early to be dealt some needed Wild Cards that may be lurking down deep in the pack. Careful analysis of the board may give you keen inklings when Five or a Kind are due and the betting, too, is a highly significant factor.

The various angles of Baseball can be nicely appreciated by considering a deal that occurred in a six-player game, in which most of the players were tight, with the exception of a keen player named Engle, from whose viewpoint the game will be described:

	Andrews	Baird	Cullen	Davis	Engle	Flick
Hole Card	*	*	*	*	(3 ♦)	*
Hole Card	*	*	*	*	(K ♥)	*
Up Card	8 ♣	J ♣	Q ♠	6 ♣	10 ♦	4 ♣
Extra Hole	—	—	—	—	—	*

Cullen opened with his high Q♠, Davis folded and Engle stayed, as did all the rest. Refer back to the list of *tight openers* and you will see that Engle had less than minimum, but he never liked to fold a hand with a wild hole card until after another round, particularly when nobody was showing a wild up card. Meanwhile, Engle was analyzing the opposition thus:

Andrews, a really tight player, had to have two Wild Cards

71

in the hole to meet his strict opening standards. Baird needed a Pair of Jacks, or a Wild Card and a high Club in the hole. Cullen, another very tight player, probably had two Queens or a Wild Card and a Queen. It was unlikely that Flick held a Wild Card in the hole, for that would mean that too many *wilds* had been dealt this soon. Probably he was satisfied with a high Pair and felt that his hand was strong because of its extra down card.

The next round resulted in:

	Andrews	Baird	Cullen	Engle	Flick
Hole Card	*	*	*	(3 ♦)	*
Hole Card	*	*	*	(K ♥)	*
Up Card	8♣	J♣	Q♠	10 ♦	4♣
Extra Hole	—	—	—	—	*
4th Card	J♠	8♥	5♥	Q♥	8♠

Andrews and Baird each got what the other wanted, so their hands were unchanged. Cullen had no use for the 5 ♥, but the Q ♥ put Engle nicely in the running. There were ten high cards that could have given him three parts to a Royal Flush or a King-high Flush in either Hearts or Diamonds, with a few Wild Cards besides, so it wasn't surprising that he hit. Engle bet his Queen-Ten and Flick, who had evidently been hoping for a high card or a wild one, promptly folded. Andrews raised. apparently happy with the Jack. Baird, Cullen and Engle stayed.

The next round brought:

	Andrews	Baird	Cullen	Engle
Hole Card	*	*	*	(3 ♦)
Hole Card	*	*	*	(K ♥)
Up Card	8♣	J♣	Q♠	10 ♦
4th Card	J♠	8♥	5♥	Q♥
5th Card	5♣	3♣	5♠	K♣

It looked as though Baird had profited most, but he turned down his hand. The reason was that even with the Wild Three, his hand wasn't good enough to match the pot in order to stay. The raise that Andrews made in the previous round spelled the difference. So Engle bet his high King; and both Andrews and Cullen stayed. Engle bet because he knew he had the highest hand, Three Kings, Cullen probably had Three Queens; and Andrews, Three Jacks, but Andrews was more dangerous because both his hole cards were probably Wild.

Cards were dealt to the remaining players, thus:

	Hole	Hole	Up Card	4th	5th	6th
Andrews	*	*	8♣	J♠	5♣	2♥
Cullen	*	*	Q♠	5♥	5♠	7♣
Engle	(3♦)	(K♥)	10♦	Q♥	K♣	10♥

Turned down by other players: **J♣ , 8♥ , 8♠ , 6♣ , 4♣ , 3♣**

Here, Engle's analysis of the hands ran thus:

His own hand, with the Wild **3♦**, gave him a Full House, K, K, K, 10, 10, which apparently was the best hand on the board, but not likely to stand up because:

Andrews with two Wild Cards in the hole, could make Four of a Kind with any of the following for a 7th card: 2 Jacks, 1 Eight, 1 Five, 3 Twos and probably 3 Wild Cards, a total of 10 chances.

Cullen, probably with a Wild Card and a Queen, could make Four of a Kind with the following: 1 Queen, 1 Five and presumably 3 Wild Cards, a total of 5 chances.

However, Engle's own chances were really better. He could make Four of a Kind with any of the following: 2 Kings, 2 Tens, a Straight Flush with the **A♥** or **J♥** and probably 3 Wild Cards, a total of 9, which with the exception of the Tens, would top anything that Andrews or Cullen could make.

There was just one problem: Cullen might actually have two Wild Cards in the hole. If so, he now had the highest hand on the board, Four Fives, which would beat Engle's Full House. But since Engle wasn't banking on his Full House (K, K, K,

10, 10) he didn't expect Cullen's low Four of a Kind (5, 5, 5, 5) to stand up either; that is, if Cullen really had them, which Engle was quite sure he didn't, because Cullen had checked his Pair of Fives earlier and hadn't raised after Engle bet.

So now, when Cullen checked again, Engle bet; and when Andrews and Cullen simply called, Engle was quite sure his analysis was right; Cullen didn't have those Four Fives. Engle hoped that each 7th card would be a dud, because then his King-high Full would win. When the seventh cards were dealt, Engle received the J ♥ face down, one of the cards he most wanted. Cullen must have gotten something, too, for he bet instead of checking. Which gave Engle new qualms regarding Cullen's possible Four Fives. Still, Engle raised. Andrews folded, Cullen called, and here is how the hands stood at the finish:

	Hole	Hole	Up card	4th	5th	6th	Down
Andrew	(3♠)	(9♣)	8♣	J♠	5♣	2♥	(6♦)
Cullen	(9♠)	(Q♦)	Q♠	5♥	5♠	7♣	(9♥)
Engle	(3♦)	(K♥)	10♦	Q♥	K♣	10♥	(J♥)

Despite his two wild hole cards, Andrews wasn't able to make Four of a Kind, which can happen quite occasionally. However, a fourth Jack — or a Wild Card — wouldn't have helped him, since Cullen hooked a Wild Card that gave him Four Queens. It was Cullen who griped because Engle was dealt the Jack that might have gone to Andrews; Engle could have used Cullen's Nine of Hearts instead, whereas the Jack of Hearts wouldn't have helped Cullen in the least.

So Engle won the pot with a Royal Flush — ♥ : A, K, Q, J, 10 (with Wild Three) over Cullen's Four Queens (with two Wild Nines). This shows that Engle knew his angles when it came to analyzing other player's holdings and calculating chances. It also shows how close and exciting a deal of Baseball can be when two or more players are going for a high Four of a Kind or something better.

Variations of Baseball

In an early form of Baseball Poker, a Three coming as an up card, meant that the player was *out* where that deal was concerned. No matter how good his hand was up to that point, he was just another loser. It may still be a good rule for those who like it, but the business of *matching the pot* puts more chips into the game and adds to its strategy.

As a compromise, a rule may be introduced whereby the deal of a Three as an up card compels everybody to match the pot or put in a specified number of chips, no mattter who receives the card. This rule is not recommended, as it favors the player who received the up card Three at the expense of all the rest.

Some people criticize the rule of giving a player an extra card when he is dealt a Four as an up card. They want the rule eliminated despite the fact that it is the most distinctive feature of the game. They claim that if a player is dealt four Fours as up cards, he has a tremendous advantage because he has seven hole cards and a total of eleven cards in all.

Actually, his four *extras* are simply the Fours themselves. He has a stronger chance than other players of having a Wild Card in the hole; in fact, he may have two or even three. But he only needs one to turn his Four Fours into Five Fours, which is the poorest Five of a Kind that he can hold, except for Five Deuces. If another player should have Four Fives as up cards and is betting them, the man with the Four Fours would do well to fold, even if he has a Wild hole card.

In short, with four Fours showing, a player is tabbed for Five Fours and nothing better. Anybody who raises him is likely to have a higher Five of a Kind. His only hope is to make a bigger Five of a Kind out of his seven down cards and forget the Fours entirely. But Five of a Kind isn't quite that easy to come by, even in this wild game.

Actually, the real advantage of receiving Fours is that the

player gains more down cards. To offset this, some groups use a rule that each extra card must be dealt face up. Another modification is to keep them face down except when a Four is dealt as a regular sixth card. Then the extra must be dealt face up. The probable reason for this variant is that since the seventh card is always dealt face down, it would be unfair to give a player the benefit of two down cards in a row at the finish of the deal.

An early and almost forgotten variant is to let a player keep or discard a Four as he chooses. If he discards it, he is dealt another card instead. He can do this with a Four as down card by simply showing it and receiving another down card in its place. If he is dealt a Four as an up card, he can call for another up card as a replacement.

Five Card Baseball

This is regular Five Card Stud, incorporating the Baseball rules: Nines and Threes wild, but the player must match the pot if he gets one as an up card. As usual, a Four as an up card gives the player an extra card, but in this case it must be dealt face up. A high Three of a Kind can win a pot in this game, but watch out for a potential Straight, Flush or Full House. Competition can be very keen, but if you hold Four of a Kind, you're pretty sure of a win. Such hands appear more often than they really should, but there are seldom two in the same deal.

Football

This is simply Baseball in a slightly different, but actually preferable form. The principal Wild Cards are the Sixes, because a touchdown counts six points in real football. Threes are wild, too, but anyone receiving one as an up card must match the pot or drop out. This is because a field goal counts three points in football, but is apt to miss. Anyone dealt a face-up Deuce is dealt an extra card, as in Baseball, because a safety counts two points in a football game, much better than using Fours (as in Baseball) because Twos are the lowest cards in the pack and therefore the most worthless; and since may Poker players are already acclimated to forms of Deuces Wild, they are easier to keep in mind than Fours.

VII

HIGH LOW POKER

A very popular form of Poker that may be played with almost any type of game. The play is as usual, but when the hands are finally declared, the player with the highest hand splits the pot with the one who holds the lowest.

Hands are rated as in standard Poker, hence the lowest card in a hand would normally be 7, 5, 4, 3, 2 of more than one suit. The highest card in the hand determines its value and a Seven is the lowest *high card* that a player can hold, as a hand running 6, 5, 4, 3, 2 would be a Straight.

In *Draw Poker*, players can stay on anything in *High Low*, so it is often hard to tell if a player is drawing for *high* or *low*, especially when he draws just one card. Pat hands, too, can be foolers.

In Seven Card High Low, the up cards are also deceptive and a player can vary his choice of final five cards to make up a high or low hand as he prefers. The same applies to Six or Eight Card High Low.

Originally, players each announced their best high or low and the pot was therewith split. Today, in most games, they must declare whether they are going after high or low. The one with the best hand in each department is the winner, but no one can switch after declaring.

Odd situations can arise with this rule. In Draw with High Low, A might go for high with 6, 6, 6, K, 8 and B might go for high with J, J, 7, 7, 5. A third player, C, holding Q, Q, 10, 10, 9 might figure that either A or B had a better high than his, so C would go for low.

In the showdown, A's three Sixes would beat B's Jacks Up for high. With B thus eliminated, C's Queens Up would be good for low, even though B held a lower Two Pair. Chances like this often encourage several players to stay in hopes of *backing in* on either high or low, thus getting half the pot.

In Seven Card High Low, a player with ♦: K, 9, 7, 4, 2, ♠: 8, 5 would have a King-high Diamond Flush for high, and an 8, 7, 5, 4, 2 for low, so he would have to use smart judgment to know which way to go. He might be beaten for high by a Full House, or for low by a hand headed by 8 and 6.

Nowadays, to make it still more exciting, in many games, a player is allowed to go for *high* and *low*. This means he is after both and if he wins them, he gets the whole pot. But if he loses either one, he loses both. The hand just given is the sort with which a player would go for *high and low*.

The best way to declare for high or low, is for each player to have a chip hidden in his fist. All are opened at once and anyone with a blue chip reveals that he is going for high; with a white chip, low. Where high and low is allowable, a player holds a red chip. Other types of markers can be used instead.

Or players can simply state high, low, or both, beginning with the first player to the dealer's left and going around the circle, including all players still in the hand.

Ace as High or Low is played a great deal nowadays. A player with a Flush would call his Ace a high card, but going for low, he would call an Ace low. With that rule, the lowest possible hand is 6, 4, 3, 2, A.

High Low Baseball

Most high low games follow the pattern of the *high* game, with special stress on *low* hands. Baseball, when played *high low* offers some tricky exceptions, which can be profitable on the right occasions. Still better, losses can be avoided, as will be seen.

High Low Baseball is usually played with a *swinging Ace* which can be classed as high or low, as the holder prefers. Each players can declare for *high* or *low* or *high* and *low*, as in most *high low games*. Those rules are helpful, so should be specified rather than other variations.

Most important in High Low Baseball is the Three penalty. If it is kept to the size of the pot, you would have to turn down practically every Three, because winning *high* or *low* would only bring back what you put in — sometimes less. So the penalty should be cut to half the size of the pot, and a limit may be set on that.

Assuming that it is a *half-pot* penalty, you still do better to turn down a Three unless it offers a good chance for *high* and *low*. If one chance dwindles, the other may come through, giving you a split. But it's best to fold unless one looks sure.

Most players regard a Four as trifling in Baseball, though nice if it gives you a face-down Three. Otherwise, you might have just as well been dealt some other card instead of the Four. That's true, where *high* hands are concerned, but in a game of *high low* a Four is valuable in its own right, as it is needed in a *low* hand. It also brings an extra hole card that may prove doubly valuable when you are going for both *high* and *low*. That worked for Doc Griffin in a hand like this:

*   *   A♦   4♥   *   A♠   3♠   *

It was a game with a big limit and two other players were betting heavily, both with good holdings. Thanks to the 4♥, Doc received a down card that kept him in the running. But, he was in a bad plight when that 3♠ showed as his final up card. The hand on Doc's left looked high:

*   *   Q♦   9♣   J♦   Q♣   *

While on his right was a low one:

*   *   2♥   5♣   9♦   J♣   *

80

Still, Doc put up a half-pot penalty for the privilege of staying with his 3♠. The man on the right bumped the pot and so did the man on the left, but being in that deep, Doc had to stay. They were dealt their final cards face down and after Doc took a close peek at his cards, he began bumping the pot along with the other players. Finally, each decided to call him; out of charity, no doubt.

Henley, on the left, announced *high* as was expected, while Dilks, on the right, went for *low*. When Doc declared *high* and *low*, they both smiled, thinking that since he knew he was licked both ways, he was trying to make a good show of it.

With that, Henley turned up his first two hole cards, which proved to be the 3♣ and the 10♦. He lined up five cards as follows: 3♣, 9♣, Q♦, J♦, 10♦.

That obviously stood for ♦: A, K, Q, J, 10. So Henley remarked, "Sorry about your Four Aces, Doc, but my Royal Flush tops them."

Dilks, by then, had turned up his first two hole cards. They were the 9♥ and the 4♣. He formed a row of five that ran: 9♥, 5♣, 4♣, 2♥, 9♦.

That represented 6,5,4,2,A. Dilks confirmed that by saying, "A sixty-five. Pretty close to a perfect low. You divide the pot, Henley, and if there's an odd buck, it goes to you for high."

Neither bothered to show his final hole card, because neither needed it. Each hand looked like a clincher on the first six cards. But their glee faded when Doc turned up his three hole cards and showed his complete hand: A♣, 2♦, A♦, 4♥, 3♦, A♠, 3♠, 8♣

Doc had gotten the 3♦ down, and when he received the 3♠ as an up card, it was just what he, as the *doctor*, had ordered. It gave him a two-way *lock*. First, he lined up these five: A♠, A♦, 3♦, A♣, 3♠

"Five Aces for high," Doc told Henley. "They're unbeatable."

Next, he removed the **A♠** and **A♦**; then added **4♥** and **2♦** to the line-up, which he arranged thus: **3♠, 4♥, 3♦, 2♦, A♣**

"That's a sixty-four," Doc told Dilks. "Six, four, three, two, ace, a perfect low in this game. Just one notch under sixty-five."

So Doc took the entire pot, which anybody could have done with a hand like that. But the hand itself depended upon that neatest of combinations, an *up* Four followed by a *down* Three. That was what kept Doc in business and put him enough ahead to buy the **3♠** when it came along.

Now for the all-important question if you plan to play High Low Baseball. Which of Doc's main opponents was most justified in standing by his guns: Henley, who went for *high* with his Royal Flush, or Dilks, who stood by his almost perfect *low* of 6,5,3,2,A?

Statistically, the Royal Flush could have been beaten by *any* Five of a Kind, from Deuces on up. Practically, that is a very difficult achievement, even in a game like Baseball. In contrast, a low of 6,5,3,2,A, which is wonderful in most *low* games, is anything but sure. Henley was right to stand on *high* with **♦: A, K, Q, J, 10.** Dilks was wrong to bank on a *low* 6,5,4,2,A, which could have been beaten by a 6,4,3,2,A.

In fact, a *perfect low* is so common in High Low Baseball that two may frequently appear in the same deal, which can be settled by dividing the low half of the split pot. As a result, many experienced players regard a Five as poison because it lures them into *low* hopes that are almost sure to lose.

In another game of High Low Baseball, Doc wisely went for *high* when four other players were after *low*. The showdown ran like this:

Doc	(A♣)	(3♦)	Q♣	10♠	9♥	7♠	(Q♥)
Andy	(6♠)	(2♠)	9♣	J♦	A♠	Q♦	(4♥)
Joey	(A♥)	(4♠)	5♦	4♣	8♥	6♥	(K♣)
	Joey's extra (3♥)						
Pete	(2♦)	(3♠)	6♦	K♥	A♦	J♥	(9♠)

Bart   (3♣) (6♣) 2♣ 8♠ 5♥ 4♦ (7♥)
           Bart's extra (5♠)

Doc was banking heavily on his final card, with strong prospects for a Royal Flush in Clubs or a Straight Flush in Spades, and needing only an Ace, Queen, Ten, or Seven for Four of a Kind. Andy's hand was the one that bothered Doc, but when Andy went *low* like the rest, Doc didn't even need the Q♥ that came as his final card. But what happend to the others was the interesting partt. They laid out their five-card hands thus:

Andy	6♠	4♥	9♣	2♠	A♠	(6-4-3-2-A)
Joey	6♥	5♦	4♣	3♥	A♥	(6-5-4-2-A)
Pete	6♦	3♠	9♠	2♦	A♦	(6-4-3-2-A)
Bart	6♣	5♥	4♦	2♣	3♣	(6-5-4-2-A)

Two players with 6, 4, 3, 2, A and two with 6, 5, 4, 2, A show how thinly it can be cut. That's why many players fold early unless they have hopes for *high* as well as *low*. When you see the game is shaping that way, you can go along with a *Sixty-five*, particularly a 6, 5, 3, 2, A (rather than a 6, 5, 4, 2, A) There are hands where a *Seventy-six* (as 7, 6, 6, 2, A) can take *low*, or even an *Eighty-seven* (as 8, 7, 5, 4, A). It's a good policy to watch for such chances.

One system is to check the Fours, because they are doubly important to a *low* hand. In a six-handed game, if all players stay, there will be at least 36 cards dealt before the final down card. Three of those should normally be Fours. If less have turned up, any player showing low cards should be figured as having a Four in the hole. When any do show up, the extra card a player gets may be his *clincher* toward a *low*. So make sure you have a possible *perfect low* against such opposition.

Any Four that comes your way may not only help your low prospect, but discount the opposing chances. A nice start is a 3, 3, 4, with two Threes tucked away as wild hole cards and giving you an extra hole card for your Four. One player started with **3 ♦ , 3 ♥ , 4♣,** and was dealt the **6♣** as an extra. Next he received the **9 ♥** and he practically clinched *high* and *low* with his second up card. His **3 ♦ , 3 ♥ , 6♣, 9 ♥ , 4♣,** gave him a Straight Flush (**♣: 8, 7, 6, 5, 4**) for high. By rearranging them (**6♣, 4♣, 3 ♦ , 3 ♥ , 9 ♥**) and calling them different suits, he had a perfect 6, 4, 3, 2, A for *low*.

That is High Low Baseball at its best!

Lowball

This is a development of Low Hand Poker in which the lowest hand wins. In its original form hands rank exactly as in regular Draw or Stud, but are valued in reverse, so that 7, 5, 4, 3, 2 of mixed suits is the best possible hand, and **♦ : A, K, Q, J, 10** is the worst. In Draw, players throw away high cards or Pairs hoping to catch low ones; while in Stud, the hand with the lowest card or cards showing is the hand that bets first.

Players may agree to count an Ace as low instead of high, so in that case — 6, 4, 3, 2, A becomes the best possible hand. This is a logical addition, as high cards have no value. Thus the highest No Pair hand would be K, Q, J, 10, 9 of mixed suits. In the case of Pairs, the lower wins, the best being A, A, 2, 3, 4 with Ace low.

Lowball, in its most developed form, has gone beyond that. It is generally played as a form of Draw Poker, Straights and Flushes being ruled out entirely. Thus 5, 4, 3, 2, A becomes the best hand, regardless of suits, and is called a *Wheel*.

The chance of such a hand on the deal is about 1 out of 2500, so a Wheel is a trophy indeed, and worth going after on a draw. In Lowball, a player may still win with a fairly good draw. If holding K, 4, 3, 2, A he could discard the King, hoping to catch a Five; yet a Six, Seven or even an Eight would keep him in the action.

Anything opens in Lowball, since players are going for low not high. The game is played extensively in western gambling casinos, which often set their own special rules.

84

VIII

Spit In The Ocean

This form of modern Poker has undergone more changes than any other games. Originally it was very simple, but as new features were introduced, it blossomed into the wildest of Wild Poker games. Today the trend has reversed itself, bringing Spit as it is termed back into the conservative fold. But since anything goes in Dealer's Choice, the best policy is to trace Spit in the Ocean through its varied career, with stops along the line.

Simple Spit in the Ocean

This is regular Draw Poker, except that each player is dealt only four cards. Then, a single card is dealt face up in the center of the table as a *common card* for all the players, making the fifth card in each player's hand. Suppose the center or common card should be the **3♣** and that you happen to hold:

K♦   J♦   3♦   3♠

All those Diamonds look nice toward a Flush, but you can't get it, because you are stuck with the **3♣** as a common card. So you discard the **K♦** and **J♦**, hoping to turn your Three Threes (**3♦, 3♠, 3♣**) into a Full House (as 3, 3, 3, J, J) or Four of a kind, yet at the same time hoping that your Three Threes will stand on their own merits.

That's practically the same as ordinary Draw Poker, except

that you are governed by the common card, which affects other players' hands as well. So to make everybody happy somebody introduced:

Spit with Center Card Wild

As in the simple game, each player is dealt four cards, with an extra in the center. But instead of representing itself, the common card is *wild*, allowing each player to call it whatever he chooses. That naturally gives him more leeway than in the simple game, as will be seen by taking the example already given with the 3♣ as a common card, and the player holding:

K♦   J♦   3♦   3♠

Here, the player could go for a Flush, by discarding the 3♠ and considering the common 3♣ to be the A♦. If he should draw any Diamond — say the Six — his hand would then stand:

A♦   K♦   J♦   6♦   3♦
(3♣)

The A♦ is represented by the *wild* center card (3♣). The player designates it as the Ace of Diamonds in order to give himself the highest possible Flush. If he had missed his Flush, a draw of a card such as the K♠ (instead of the 6♦) would have given him Three of a Kind, thus:

King   K♦   K♠   J♦   3♦
(3♣)

Here, the "wild" card would have represented any King, with no need to name the actual suit. Similarly, if he had drawn a card like the J♣ (instead of the 6♦) he could class his hand as Three Jacks, thus:

Jack   J♦   J♣   K♦   3♦
(3♣)

Although the center card is wild, this form of Spit cannot properly be classed as a *wild game* because all players have an equal opportunity to use the wild card, with no chance of picking up another. Therefore, the game can be treated like regular Draw Poker, but due to the presence of the wild center card, the hands will run consistently higher, as follows:

In Draw Poker (Standard Game)		In Spit (Center Card Wild)
An Unpaired Hand	becomes	One Pair
K, 10, 8, 4	+ Wild =	K, K, 10, 8, 4
A One Pair Hand	becomes	Three of a Kind
8, 8, J, 5	+ Wild =	8, 8, 8, J, 5
A Two Pair Hand	becomes	A Full House
J, J, 7, 7	+ Wild =	J, J, J, 7, 7
Three of a Kind	becomes	Four of a Kind
9, 9, 9, 3	+ Wild =	9, 9, 9, 9, 3
Four of a Kind	becomes	Five of a Kind
6, 6, 6, 6	+ Wild =	6, 6, 6, 6, 6

Note that Straights, Flushes, and Straight Flushes are not included in the table, because their value is not increased. They are easier to get; that's all. If you are dealt the **K ♥, Q ♦, J ♦, 10 ♥**, you will have an Ace-high Straight, because when the spit card is turned up, you simply call it an Ace. Similarly, if you are dealt the **A ♣, K ♣, 5 ♣, 2 ♣**, you will have a Club Flush, because you name the *spit* card as the **Q ♣**. The same applies where a Straight Flush is concerned.

Remember, however, that your easy-to-get Straight or easy-to-get Flush can be beaten by what ordinarily would have been Two Pair, but is now a Full House; or by a standard Three of a Kind which now rates as Four of a Kind. Also, a Straight Flush, if you get one, can be topped by Five of a Kind. However, if you hold three parts toward a Straight Flush, a one card draw is excellent. For example, with the **5 ♦** as a wild center card, you might hold:

Q♣ J♣ 10♣ 7♦

Discarding the 7♦, a draw of the **A♣, K♣, 9♣** or **8♣** would give you a Straight Flush, thanks to the Wild **5♦**. That would beat any *Fours* or *Fulls* that anyone else might hold. There are six Clubs, good for a Flush and twelve Aces, Kings, Nines and Eights that could give you a Straight, thus beating a Three of a Kind. In addition, there are nine Queens, Jacks and Tens, which could give you Three of a Kind that might be higher than anyone else's.

In contrast, suppose the **8♥** is the Wild Card in the center and you hold:

Q♠ Q♦ J♥ 10♣

There are sixteen cards (4 As, 4 Ks, 4 9s and 4 8s) that can fill a Straight; but to draw one, you will have to discard a Queen, so you run the risk of sacrificing high triplets (Q, Q, Q) which you already hold. So in this case, it's good judgment to hold your Queens and draw two cards, on the chance that you will pick up another Pair, giving you a Full House with the Wild Card (as 8, Q, Q, 4, 4) or that you may catch another Queen for Four of a Kind (8, Q, Q, Q, 7).

Spit: Center Value Wild

This is an extremely wild game that has become so popular among groups favoring wild play that they refer to it as Spit in the Ocean as if it were the original game as well as the one and only. However, to be sure that everyone understands, this type of *Spit* should be declared beforehand. As usual, the center card, or "spit" is wild; and so are *all others of that value* which happen to be held by individual players.

Thus if the **3♣** happen to be the common card, the following situations would arise:

With **K♦, J♣, 8♥, 5♣**, you would have a Pair of Kings (**K♦** and **3♣**).

With **K♦**, **J♣**, **8♥**, **3♦**, you would have Three Kings (**K♦**, **3♦**, **3♣**).

With **K♦**, **J♣**, **3♠**, **3♦**, you would have Four Kings (**K♦**, **3♠**, **3♦**, **3♣**).

With **K♦**, **3♥**, **3♠**, **3♦**, you would have Five Kings (**K♦**, **3♥**, **3♠**, **3♦**, **3♣**).

That sounds wild enough, but it by no means exhausts the possibilities. In this game, it is quite possible for one player to hold 10, 10, 3, 3 against another's 9, 9, 9, 3, with a "3" as the *spit*, common to both hands, so that with the showdown, the player with Five Tens (10, 10, 3, 3; Spit = 10, 10, 10, 10, 10) would triumph over the player with the Five Nines (9, 9, 9, 3, Spit = 9, 9, 9, 9, 9) by the narrowest of margins.

In this crazy game, you shoot for Four of a Kind; and in a six-player game, one is likely to show up in nearly every deal. Hence Straights and Flushes can be generally disregarded and even a Full House is apt to prove futile. A player holding two Wild Cards in his hand often has an advantage over an opponent who has a strong holding in *natural* cards, as is evidenced by the following example, in which the *spit* was the **9♥**:

Player A   Q♥ Q♦ Q♣ 5♣
Player B   9♦ 9♠ 10♥ 7♣

With Player A betting heavily on Four Queens, Player B began wondering if his Four Tens were high enough to win. So when Player A discarded a single card, Player B threw away the **10♥** and **7♣**, drawing to his Wild Cards only. Player A naturally discarded the **5♣** and picked up the **K♣**, which didn't help him, while Player B drew the **6♠** and **2♠**, which looked worse than those he had discarded. But by calling the **9♦** the **5♠**; the **9♠**, the **4♠**; and the **9♥**, the **3♠**, he formed his hand into a Straight Flush, 6, 5, 4, 3, 2 in Spades, and won the pot with the greatest of ease.

Usually in this ultra-wild game, players are limited to a draw of three cards each, which lessens a player's chances of

89

drawing a Wild Card and also makes a seven-player game very effective. The same rule can be applied to the more conservative forms of Spit.

Five Card Spit

In this early form of Spit in the Ocean, each player is dealt five cards face down. Then a sixth card is turned face up to establish a wild value for that deal; but this card is an *indicator only* and does not figure in the play. All other cards of that value are wild, however, so there are three such cards instead of four. Play proceeds exactly as in Draw Poker and the game is very much like Deuces Wild, except that there are only three Wild Cards instead of four, which decreases the chances of big hands proportionately. Players are usually limited to a draw of three cards.

Some students of Poker lore have traced Spit in the Ocean back to the days when an odd card was dealt face down ; then turned up after to determine the Wild value. Since this left the pack one Wild Card short, that situation was rectified by letting the dealer designate the wild denomination, naming whatever value he wanted, as described under the general head of Wild Games.

Meanwhile, however, Spit had taken hold and continued to be played partly because of the mystery element. In those days, the standard pack contained only one Joker, so it was sometimes added to take the place of the card turned up as the Spit. Thus if the 5 ♦ happened to turn up, the wild cards in the pack would be the **5♠, 5♣, 5♥** and Joker, so the chances would be the same as the Deuces Wild.

Pig in Poke

This is another name for Five Card Spit with the turned up

card representing Pig in Poke which establishes the three Wild Cards or four with Joker — exactly as described in Five Card Spit. However, the game can be stepped up with another feature that stresses the Pig in Poke. Each player is dealt only four cards; then the Spit is turned up and a round of betting follows. Each player bets on the prospects for his four cards but the Spit or Pig in Poke is an indicator only and forms no part of his hand.

After that round a fifth card is dealt to each player and the hands are bet exactly as in Five Card Spit. Following that, players draw in the usual fashion and a third and final betting round transpires. The extra betting round peps up the game, as Straights and Flushes are strong hands (just as in Deuces Wild) so if a player's first four cards indicate such prospects, he can afford to bet heavily. Even better, Two Pair on his first four cards will give him ideas regarding a Full House, which a Wild Card could fill even before the draw!

It is easy to see how this game represents a transition from Five Card Spit to the more popular four-card versions described at the outset of this chapter; and the same applies still further with the variant called:

Wild Widow

Usually, this term has been used interchangeably with Pig in the Poke, with the extra card termed a Widow and establishing the value of the Wild Cards in the hands. However, Wild Widow can be carried farther, adding a new touch to the game. A Widow, in most card games, represents a card, or cards that can be added to a player's hand, enabling him to discard something in its place. Applying this rule in the present case, each player would be allowed to substitute the extra card for one already in his hand; *not* as a Wild Card, but *as itself*.

Offhand, that option would seem trifling indeed. Suppose you found yourself with the following cards:

Your Hand: 4♦   A♥   A♣   J♣   7♣
     Widow: 4♠

With the 4♦ wild, you already hold Three Aces, so if you discard the J♣ and 7♣, you will have two chances of drawing one of four cards — 4♣, 4♥, A♠, A♦, that will give you Four Aces. However, if you discard the A♥ and draw a single card, it would allow eleven chances for a Club Flush. Since the 4♦, already in your hand, can be classed as a Club, you can fill the Flush by drawing the 4♥ or 4♣, as well as any of following: K♣, Q♣, 10♣, 9♣, 8♣, 6♣, 5♣, 3♣, 2♣.

Still, many players would prefer to hold the two Aces on the chance of getting those big Four Aces, with possibilities of Five of a Kind, or a Full House, because of the two-card draw. But obviously, the Widow Card, would be of no help whatever to your hand, if simply considered as itself. So it would have no influence upon your decision.

Now, study this contrasting case:

Your Hand: 10♦   Q♠   Q♥   9♥   5♠
     Widow: 10♥

Here, as in the previous hand, you can go for Four Queens by holding the 10♦, Q♠, Q♥ and junking the 9♥ and 5♠. You have the same chance as before of catching the 10♣, 10♠, Q♦ or Q♣. If any of those should show up in your two-card draw, all would be fine. Suppose however, that instead of discarding the 9♥ and the 5♠, you kept the 9♥ and let the 5♠ go. You would still have half as good a chance of getting your Four Queens (by picking up the 10♣, 10♠, Q♦ or Q♣ in one draw instead of two); in addition, you would have the following chances of improving your hand by a one card draw!

If you draw the 9♠, 9♣ or 9♦, you will have a *Full House* — Q, Q, Q, 9, 9 — *with the Wild* 10♦ rating as a Queen.

If you draw the King, Queen or Jack of Hearts, you can count the 10♥ as part of your hand instead of the Q♠. Thanks to the Wild **10♦**, you will then have a *Straight Flush* in Hearts, running ♥: K, Q, J, 10, 9 or ♥: Q, J, 10, 9, 8, as the case may be.

If you draw any other Heart — A, 7, 6, 5, 4, 3, 2 — simply count the **10♥** instead of the **Q♠** and call the Wild **10♦** a Heart, which will give you an *Ace-high Heart Flush*.

· If you draw a King, Jack or Eight of any suit besides Hearts, you can form a Straight — K, Q, J, 10, 9, or Q, J, 10, 9, 8 in exactly the same fashion as the *Straight Flush*.

In all, your chances of improvement come to $4 + 3 + 3 + 7 + 9 = 26$ out of a possible 46 cards, which is considerably better than an even break.

IX

MIXED TYPES
OF POKER

During the period when Seven Card Stud and Spit in the Ocean were gaining favor among Poker addicts, it became increasingly evident that their numerous offshoots would eventually take on an interwoven pattern, each borrowing essential features from the other. Such *hybrid games* as these might be termed, not only did develop, but became a distinct category of their own. They run the gamut from conservative games to those that are really wild, thus allowing a wide range when playing Dealer's Choice. Many of the more popular are described herewith, beginning with what may be considered the progenitor of the parade.

Round The World

Each player is dealt a hand of four down cards with a card turned up in the center of the table, being regarded as a part of each player's hand, exactly as in Spit. A round of betting follows, but the players do not draw as in Spit. Instead, another card is dealt face up alongside the first and there is another round of betting, as in Stud, with the second up card belonging to all hands. A third up card is dealt, also on a mutual basis, followed by a betting round; then a fourth, on which the players also bet.

Thus each player has a choice of eight cards in all; four in his own hand and four as common cards, which appear in a face-up row. With the showdown, the highest five card hand wins, as in standard Poker.

To illustrate: the center cards are shown at the top, in the order in which they were turned up, so keep that in mind when reading the comments. Below are the six hands held by the players:

	1st	2nd	3rd	4th
Center	3♠	6♦	J♠	9♦
Anna	A♠	Q♠	9♠	3♥
Bess	K♣	J♣	3♣	6♥
Cleo	J♥	9♣	4♥	4♣
Dora	K♥	Q♦	10♠	5♣
Elsa	A♣	8♣	10♦	10♥
Fran	K♠	K♦	9♥	4♠

First Round: With the turn up of the **3♠**, Anna opens on the strength of a Four Flush; A♠, Q♠, 9♠, (3♠). Bess stays with three parts toward a Flush; K♣, J♣, 3♣. Cleo tags along on a Pair of Fours; 4♥, 4♣. So does Dora, with three parts toward a Straight; K♥, Q♦, 10♠. Elsa likes her Pair of Tens; 10♦, 10♥. Fran is almost inclined to raise on a Pair of Kings; K♠, K♦, but decides to wait, which is fortunate, or Anna might have raised it further with her prospect of an Ace-high Flush. In which case, some of the others might have dropped. As it is, everybody stays.

Second Round: Turned up cards are now **3♠, 6♦**.

Anna bets, still looking for a Flush. Bess stays on her Pair of Sixes; 6♥, (6♦). The rest still stay. Only Bess has improved and she might have dropped otherwise.

Third Round: Turned Up: **3♠, 6♦, J♠**

Anna has her Flush, A♠, Q♠, (J♠), 9♠, (3♠), so she bets,

hoping that some of the others have good hands, but not better! Bess stays with Two Pair; J♣, (J♠), 6♥, (6♦) and high hopes of a Full House. Cleo also stays on Two Pair; J♥, (J♠), 4♥, 4♣. Dora stays on a bobtail Straight; K♥, Q♦, (J♠), 10♠. Both Elsa and Fran stay, but they would have dropped if anyone had raised Anna.

Fourth Round: Turned up: 3♠, 6♦, J♠, 9♦

Anna checks her Flush, hoping someone is strong enough to bet. Bess checks with her Two Pair. So does Cleo, whose Two Pair now rate J♥, (J♠), 9♣, (9♦). Dora takes the bait and bets the limit on the Straight that she has just acquired; K♥, Q♦, (J♠), 10♠, (9♦). Elsa folds on her unimproved Pair of Tens. Fran stays, with her high Two Pair; K♠, K♦, 9♥, (9♦), thinking they might hold up.

Anna promptly raises, whereupon Bess and Cleo drop. Dora studies the board and doubts that Anna has either a Spade or Diamond Flush. So Dora raises, hoping Anna is stuck with a low Straight. Fran folds and Anna raises and Dora, swept by misgivings, decides to call, rather than be bluffed. So Anna's Flush wins over Dora's Straight.

Note: As indicated in the description, the center cards are often dealt at the start, forming a face-down row, with cards being turned up singly. Some groups introduce a round of betting before the first center card is turned up, but that is not the usual rule. It applies more often with the next game on the list:

Cincinnati

In this highly popular outgrowth of Round the World, each player is dealt five cards to start, giving each a valid Poker hand. A row of five cards is then dealt face down in the center and the players bet on the strength of their hands. The first center card is turned up and is common to all hands. After a round of betting, the next is turned up and bets follow; then the next, and so on. Thus, each player has a total of ten cards from which to form his final hand, instead of only eight, as in Round the World.

Here is a sample hand of Cincinnati:

	1st	2nd	3rd	4th	5th
Center	7♠	3♥	Q♣	7♥	9♥
Anna	K♠	Q♦	7♣	6♣	6♥
Bess	Q♠	J♥	9♣	5♣	2♥
Cleo	A♣	J♣	J♠	8♠	2♠
Dora	K♣	10♠	10♦	4♥	3♣
Elsa	A♠	A♥	K♦	J♦	4♣
Fran	10♣	8♣	6♠	4♠	2♦

These hands run consistently higher than those shown with the sample of Round the World, due to the presence of a fifth card in each hand as well as the center layout. Anna wins with a Full House; 7♣, (7♠), (7♥), Q♦, (Q♣). Bess is next with a Flush: J♥, (9♥), (7♥), (3♥), 2♥. Fran holds a Straight; 10♣, (9♥), 8♣, (7♠), 6♠.

A Flush is strong stuff in Round the World and a Straight will often stand up in that game; but in Cincinnati, a Full House is frequently the winner. If you see three cards of one suit showing on the board, it's almost a sure sing that somebody is holding a Flush in Cincinnati, while any Pair of up cards means that a Full House is a likely prospect. If Two Pair or Triplets show among the layout cards, you'd better not stay with anything short of a Full House; and a high one at that!

Tennessee

This game is practically the same as Cincinnati, the only difference being that in Tennessee, the layout cards are dealt from the top of the pack, a new card prior to each betting interval, with each card being turned face up as it is dealt. This is at variance with the Cincinnati procedure, where the center cards are dealt in a face-down row to start and are later turned up one by one. In Tennessee, the cards have to be dealt in a row anyway, in order to keep track of them, so it amounts to the same thing.

No matter how the cards are dealt, the game can be played on a *high low* basis, as described in the section covering High Low Poker. Here is a sample hand, shown beneath a center layout, illustrating how the player would proceed:

	1st	2nd	3rd	4th	5th
Center	8♥	J♣	3♦	5♦	J♥
Hand	10♥	7♣	4♥	2♦	K♥

For his high hand, the player forms a Heart Flush by indicating the Hearts in order; for his low hand, he simply lines up the lowest cards accordingly, with these results:

High	K♥	(J♥)	10♥	(8♥)	4♥
Low	7♣	(5♦)	4♥	(3♦)	2♦

Lame Brain

Generally speaking, this is another term for Cincinnati, but Lame Brain is more frequently used to designate a wild version of the regular game. The implication is that Cincinnati is reasonably conservative and predictable, so that any one who tries to improve it by introducing wild innovations is a trifle lame in the brain. Whether that criticism is justified is somewhat irrelevant, since wild spinoffs of Cincinnati are definitely here to stay and should be accepted accordingly.

The only problem is one of nomenclature. Various titles have been given to different forms of Lame Brain, often dependent on where some particular variant originally developed. But the same game may be known by another title elsewhere; and some of the more popular names have become interchangeable. So to avoid confusion, when playing Dealer's Choice, it is best to refer to the game not only by its current title, but as "Lame Brain with lowest center card wild, with others of the same value," or whatever other rule may apply. That brings us directly to a case in point:

Cincinnati Liz or
Lame Brain Pete

Known by both titles, this is played like Cincinnati, but with the lowest center card wild, as are all others of the same value. Thus if a Deuce should turn up as the first or even the second Wild Card, players could bet rather freely, knowing that the strength of their hands would not be subject to sudden change; but if only high cards should appear, players are apt to hold back, in case something lower pops up to alter the wild situation.

Here is a good example of what can happen:

	1st	2nd	3rd	4th	
Center	J♠	8♠	7♦	4♣	
Hand	K♣	10♣	6♠	3♠	3♣

(One more card to come)

With the turn up of the first center card (J♠), it seemed almost certain that something lower would be due, so the first round of betting was light. The same applied to the second round (8♠) as was proven when the third round came still lower (7♦) and everybody stayed for the fourth round, including the player whose hand appears above, even though his hopes were by no means high.

With the turn up of the 7♦, our player clinched a Spade Flush running ♠: A, J, 8, 6, 3 with the 7♦ representing the A♠, but he knew that a Flush might be small picking in a game like this, so he was hoping for something better, such as a Full House. The 4♣ as fourth card, simply supplanted the 7♦ as *low card,* so his status remained the same.

Betting now became heavy as everybody expected the 4♣ to stand as low; and this indicated that some players had a Four in hand. Out player stayed, not on the strength of his Flush, which he didn't think would win; but on the chance that the fifth and final card might pair up with a King, Jack, Ten, Eight, Seven or Six, all of which were in his hand, or showing on the board. That would give him Two Pair (thanks to his Pair of Threes) and with the 4♣ as a Wild Card, his top Pair would become Triplets, making his hand a Full House which just might manage to win.

So he hung on and was glad he did, for to everyone's surprise, including his own, the fifth card proved to be the 3♦. so that Threes took over as *low* instead of Fours; and there was our hero, already equipped with a Pair of Threes. Take a look at the final setup:

	1st	2nd	3rd	4th	5th
Center	J♠	8♠	7♦	4♣	3♦
Hand	K♣	10♣	6♠	3♠	3♣

With three Wild Threes, our player could revise his Spade Flush to read J, 3, 3, 8, 3 which would become ♠: **J, 10, 9, 8, 7** for a Straight Flush. But he could do even better with Clubs by piecing together 3, K, 3, 3, 10 which became ♣: **A, K, Q, J, 10** for a Royal Flush in Clubs that won the pot hands down.

For still more suspense, try:

Utah

This is Cincinnati, *with the last card wild,* which means that all others of its value are wild as well. In this game, it is customary to turn up the card at the left end of the row; then the card at the right; next left, next right, leaving the middle card to the last. Here is a sample hand:

100

	1st	3rd	last	4th	2nd
Layout	K♣	10♥	7♠	2♠	7♣
Hand	K♥	J♠	7♦	5♣	3♦

In the first betting round, following the turn up of the **K♣**, our player stayed on his Pair of Kings **K♥**, (**K♣**). The turn up of the **7♣** gave him Two Pair; **K♥**, (**K♣**), **7♦**, (**7♣**), so he stayed for that round, too. Turn ups of **10♥** and **2♠** were of no immediate help, but our player was sure of a Full House before turning up the last card, because *any* value not in his hand, or showing (namely, A, Q, 9, 8, 6, 4) would be a Wild Card, giving him his "Full" of K, K, K, 7, 7. Meanwhile, if he matched a single card in either his hand or on the board (as J, 10, 5, 3, 2) he would have two Wild Cards, turning his Kings into Four of a Kind.

However, as the board shows, the turn up, of the **7♠** gives our player *three* wild cards in the form of Sevens, so he reverts to thoughts of a Flush or better and lines up his hand thus: **7♠**, **K♥**, **7♣**, **7♦**, **10♥**, and since a Seven can be anything, that gives him **♥: A, K, Q, J, 10** for a Royal Flush! That would be pretty hard to beat, except that our player already has it beaten, if he will give his hand a closer look. Since he already has two Kings (**K♥** and **K♣**) all he has to do is call each Seven a King, giving him Five Kings (K,K,K,K,K). To beat that, another player would need Three Aces in his hand, to go along with the two Wild Sevens on the board, to make a hand of five Aces. He could also do it with a Pair of Aces and the **7♥** in his hand; so Five Kings is not a "sure-win" hand, but it is very close to it.

Other Forms of Cincinnati

Many variants are possible with Cincinnati, most of them unnamed, but all allowable, if the rules are properly specified. Thus the dealer may announce, *Cincinnati, with first up card wild* or *second up card wild* — and so on according to his whim. Similarly, he may specify, *with high up card wild,* instead of *low up card wild* as in Cincinnati Liz. One popular form is to declare the lowest card in each player's hand as wild for that player only, along with any cards like it in the layout. This can produce some very unusual hands, making it difficult for other players to figure just how they stand.

Cincinnati and kindred games can also be played *high low,* like other games described under that head. This can be on the basis of high and low splitting the pot, each player forming a single hand from his own cards and the center row; or players may be allowed to form two hands — one *high* and the other *low* — thus going for both. This, of course, is a matter of Dealer's Choice. In brief, any rules generally applicable to games of the Spit or Stud type, can be used with Cincinnati, provided they are kept within feasible limits. But as a final note in this category, consider:

Hollywood

It's a long trip from Cincinnati to Hollywood, so in piling up mileage, you increase the center row as well. Each player is dealt a hand of five cards; then two rows of five each — ten cards in all — are dealt in the center and turned up for each betting round. To speed the action, turn ups may be in pairs; one from each row; but however you play it, each person has fifteen cards to choose from at the finish — his own hand, plus ten up cards. Nothing under a Flush really counts in this game, and stronger hands like Full Houses are usually the winners, but are sometimes hard to get. Wild Cards are not recommended in this game. However:

Hollywood is peculiarly adaptable to the newer games of Six Card Poker and Seven Card Poker, described under their own heads, in which case, Deuces and also Jokers are used as Wild Cards.

102

X

CROSSOVER OR CROSS WIDOW

Here is an entire group of games based on Cincinnati, but with a distinctive feature of their own. It seems to have been invented accidentally when players began dealing the center cards in a cross formation instead of a straight line. Each player had his regular hand and the center cards were then turned up in clockwise order, as left, top, right, bottom, and finally the center card. This was especially suitable to Lame Brain, in which the center card is wild, and the cross-formation reminded the dealer that the center card should be turned up last.

So far, the game differed slightly from Cincinnati, but the term Crossover was used to identify it; and Cross Widow became even more applicable, as the five cards in the center, common to all hands, are actually a widow and they are arranged in the form of a cross. Someone then decided to make competition keener by using the cross formation to limit each player's choice of widow cards. For practical purposes, this can be termed:

Crossover

Deal the five card layout in cross-formation and turn up the cards as described; but the center card is *not* wild and instead of regarding all five cards as part of his hand, he is limited to one row — either horizontal or vertical — giving him the choice of only *three* cards. This means a total of eight, five from the player's hand, three from the layout, instead of the usual ten.

Here is an example of Crossover, or Simple Criss Cross, as the game is also termed:

		Widow			
		Q♦			
	3♠	8♠	K♠		
		Q♥			
Jay	A♣	9♣	J♦	7♠	6♠
Jim	J♠	10♥	9♦	3♣	2♣
Joe	A♠	J♣	10♦	5♦	5♠
Jud	Q♣	10♠	8♥	6♦	4♣

Jay, holding two Spades, naturally uses the horizontal row with his hand, making up a Spade Flush; K♠, 8♠, 7♠, 6♠, 3♠. So he bets strongly on the center card.

Jim, who has only one Spade, looks for the prospects of a Straight and finds one; Q♦, J♠, 10♥, 9♦, 8♠, by using the vertical row and the first three cards in his hand.

Joe, with A♠ and 5♠ in his hand, uses the horizontal row and fills an Ace-high Flush; A♠, K♠, 8♠, 5♠, 3♠.

Jud has what seems practically a *nothing* hand, but which turns out to be a real *sleeper*. Holding the Q♣ and 8♥, he takes the vertical row and builds his hand into a winning Full House: Q, Q, Q, 8, 8.

Analyzing this hand, Jim definitely should drop with his Straight, because three Spades showing in the vertical row, make it all too likely that somebody held a Flush. Jay might also be smart to drop, because a rival Flush would probably beat him, as the K♠ and 8♠ are common cards, so a Flush with anything higher than Jay's 7♠ would top his hand. Joe, with his Ace-high Flush would have good reason to stay, but that Pair of Queens showing in the vertical row should make him wary of a Full House. He should drop if Jud raises on the final card, unless he knows Jud to be a chronic bluffer.

Criss Cross
(Center Card Wild)

Though the term Criss Cross is occasionally applied to the simple form of Crossover as just described, it more frequently denotes the same game with the center card wild, along with all others of the same value. However, it is best to specify this when playing Dealer's Choice. When announcing Crossover or Criss Cross, the dealer should add, *with nothing wild* or *with center value wide,* so there can be no doubt.

This game is much more volatile than the simpler version and all wild values count, whether in the layout or in a player's hand. Taking the sample layout given under Crossover, along with the same hands held by Jay, Jim, Joe and Jud respectively, the situation would shape up thus:

Jay's Flush would be Ace-high (the 8♠ serving as the A♠). By adhering to the vertical row, Jim counts the 8♠ as a King and forms a King-high Straight (K, Q, J, 10, 9). He would like to call that row Three Queens toward a Full House, but unfortunately, he can't add a Pair of Threes, because although he has a 3♣ in his hand, the 3♠ on the board is in the wrong row. Joe, however, is better off. He uses the vertical row for Three Queens (Q♦, Q♥ and wild 8♠) and adds the 5♦ and 5♠ from his hand for his Full House.

Jud still could shade Joe's *Full* of Q, Q, Q, 7, 7, with a slightly higher Q, Q, Q, 8, 8 of his own, but he doesn't have to worry over such trifles. Since both Eights are Wild (8♠ in the center and 8♥ in his hand), he calls them *Queens* and wins the pot with Five Queens, a permissible hand when Wild Cards are in play. So don't count on a Full House winning in this game.

Four of a Kind is safer, but often may be topped by a Straight Flush, which in turn will succumb to an occasional Five of a Kind.

Fiery Cross

This is Crossover or Simple Criss Cross played for High Low without any wild cards. In some circles, this is regarded as standard Criss Cross, but this should be understood beforehand; the dealer specifying Criss Cross High Low, or describing Fiery Cross as Criss Cross High Low. Hands rated and evaluated as in any form of High Low Stud (described under that head), but due to the cross arrangement, the following variants may be introduced:

(1) The simple form, in which each player makes up a High Hand and a Low Hand, using either row of the cross. The player with the high hand shares the pot with the player who has the low hand. A player with both *high* and *low* takes the entire pot. For example:

Layout

                 6♦

       3♣   8♠   8♥

                10♣

Hand: K♥   Q♥   6♥   5♥   4♦

Here, by using the horizontal bar of the cross, the player can form both High and Low. His *high* would be a Heart Flush; K♥, Q♥, 8♥, 6♥, 5♥. His *low* would be 8, 6, 5, 4, 3.

(2) In another form, which produces some interesting complexities, a player must make up his *high* from one row of the cross and his *low* from the other. In the example, the player would still use his the horizontal row to fill his King-high Heart Flush. But with his *low,* he would then be forced to use the vertical row, so the best he could do would be 10, 8, 6, 5, 4 (instead of 8, 6, 5, 4, 3).

(3) This game can be played as High Low, with each player

announcing which he is going for and using either row to make up his hand. If desired, the feature of going for *both* high and low can be included, as described under High Low Stud, with the reminder that a player going for both *must make both* in order to win. Also, players must agree beforehand whether it is permissible to make both *high* and *low* from a single row, or whether each must come from a different row. The latter course — each from a different row — is preferable, as it makes for a sharper game.

As a case in point, take this close contest between two players, Walt and Will, in a game of Fiery Cross with the Swinging Ace rule, making an Ace either high or low:

	Layout			
	5 ♦			
	J ♥	4 ♦	6 ♠	
	J ♣			
Walt	Q ♣	7 ♠	6 ♦	3 ♦	2 ♠
Will	K ♠	3 ♠	2 ♦	2 ♥	A ♥

Each went for both high and low and each laid down his hand triumphantly, gesturing to one row and saying *High;* then to the other and saying, *Low.* Each was starting to gather in the pot when the other stopped him; and suddenly, to their consternation, they found that they had each other beaten.

For *high,* Walt used the vertical row and announced a Straight consisting of **7♠, 6♦, 5♦, 4♦, 3♦.** For *low,* he used the horizontal row, announcing **7♠, 6♠, 4♦, 3♦, 2♠.**

Will also used the vertical row for *high,* forming a Straight that ran **5♦, 4♦, 3♠, 2♥, A♥;** but his 5, 4, 3, 2, A couldn't quite match Walt's 7, 6, 5, 4, 3. However, Will's low, using the horizontal row, ran **6♠, 4♦, 3♠, 2♦, A♥;** so his 6, 4, 3, 2, A was lower than Walt's 7, 6, 4, 3, 2.

So both lost and the pot went to two other players: Lou, who stayed for *high* only, with Two Pair, Aces over Eights; and Tom who trailed along for *low* with an 8, 7, 5, 4, 2. Neither should have won, yet you can't blame Walt and Will for playing it as they did. This is one game where it's best to play it both ways when the chances really look good.

Iron Cross

This is an occasional term for Crossover played for *high* only, but with each player's lowest card wild, along with all of that value. As usual, a player can only use one row of the layout to go with his hand. As an example:

	Layout				
		3♥			
	6♣	10♣	8♦		
		3♣			
Smith	K♣	10♠	10♥	9♦	8♠
Jones	Q♠	Q♥	8♥	5♠	3♠

With nothing wild, the horizontal row would give Smith a Full House, 10, 10, 10, 8, 8, beating Jones' Full of 3, 3, 3, Q, Q which is made with the vertical row. But what a difference a few wild cards make! Smith's two Eights, being wild, become Tens, giving him Five Tens, only to be beaten by Jones, whose low Three gives him three Wild Threes, which become Queens, giving him a hand of Five Queens.

In addition to the games just described, there is a similar group which comes under the general heading of:

Southern Cross

This could very properly be called Nine Card Crossover, because that is its basic form. Instead of dealing only five cards in face-up formation, nine are used thus,

```
              *
              *
      *   *   *   *   *
              *
              *
```

This gives the player five extra cards (vertical, or horizontal, as he chooses) in addition to the five in his hand, for a total of ten in all.

Southern Cross may also be played as Nine Card Criss Cross, with the center card wild, along with others of its value; also as Nine Card Fiery Cross, which is played High Low without wild cards; or as Nine Card Iron Cross with each player's lowest card wild for his hand only, along with others of its value.

Bedsprings

Each player is dealt five cards face-down; then ten cards are dealt in two columns of five each. Those on the left are turned up singly, with betting on each; then those on the right are turned up card by card in the same manner. Each player can then pick one pair of cards lying side by side as additions to his hand; but no more.

Example: A player has **Q♣, J♦, 10♦, 8♥, 5♦**

The columns run:

4♣	**Q♠**
9♠	**8♠**
8♣	**4♥**
6♦	**3♦**
2♣	**A♥**

The **9♠** gives the player an immediate Straight — Q, J, 10, 9, 8 — but with the deal of the second column, he finds he can do better by using the **6♦** and **3♦**, which are side by side, giving him a Diamond Flush, running **♦: J, 10, 6, 5, 3.**

Note: For convenience, the ten card layout can be dealt in horizontal rows instead of vertical columns. In that case, the cards in the upper row are turned up first, and corresponding cards of the lower row are paired off with them.

Twin Beds

This is Bedsprings on a more liberal scale. After the deal, the top cards of each column are turned up simultaneously and betting follows; then the next two cards, with bets; and so on until all are up. But in choosing cards to go with those he holds, a player can take any card from one column, giving him a choice of five in all, with the other column ruled out, so far as his hand is concerned.

Twin Beds Gone Wild

Various wild games have developed from Twin Beds, the simplest being to declare each head card wild for its particular column, with all others of the same value, wild whether in a player's hand or in either column. To add to the suspense, it is preferable to turn up the bottom cards of each column first; then the next two above; and so on, keeping the head cards until last.

However, the game just described can prove overly wild, with ten layout cards to pick from and two wild values. Hence many groups limit each player to a single column, with its head card the only wild one allowable for his hand as well as the column. This keeps the game within bounds, so to speak.

Twin Beds — Roll Them Over

In Twin Beds as so far described, there are five betting rounds, each following the turn up of two cards from each column. In Roll Them Over, there are four more rounds. Each player picks a card from his hand and lays it face up on the table when the dealer orders Roll. Whoever has the highest hand, combined with cards showing in the layout, is first to bet, as in Stud. Each player lays a second card face up; then a third and a fourth, with a round of bets for each, on the same high-hand basis. His last card is laid face down during the final round, and after all bets are called; it is turned face up, like the hole card in Five Card Stud, to finalize the hand.

Popular Forms of Twin Beds

Perhaps the most popular form of Twin Beds is the High Low game, with players declaring for high, low or both, as described under High Low Poker. It's best with Roll Them Over, making the declarations after the final roll. A player can form both high and low from either column. Of course it can be played in the simpler form of merely comparing hands and splitting the pot between the highest *high* and lowest *low*.

To speed the action a bit, any form of Twin Beds can be played with only four cards dealt to each player as an individual hand.

XI

SEVEN CARD SPIT

This is an over all term for a comparatively new group of games which are actually forms of Seven Card Stud, borrowing the center card feature from Spit in the Ocean primarily to speed the action and accomodate more players. However, as with all such innovations, this resulted in new variations which took on individualities of their own. Let's take a look at them.

Seven Card Mutual

This is regular Seven Card Stud with one notable exception. After each player is dealt two down cards, the next card is dealt face up on the table to serve as everybody's first up card. Players bet according to their hole cards and the mutual up card; then three more up cards are dealt in the same fashion, making four mutual up cards in all, each followed by a betting round. Finally, each player is dealt another down card, as in Seven Card Stud and there is one more betting round, after which each player shows his best five cards, This game can accomodate as many as sixteen players, with three hole cards each and four mutual up cards in the center. Bets are made in rotation from the dealer's left.

Omaha

This is patterned after Seven Card Mutual, but with two

points of difference. After each player is dealt two down cards, there is an immediate betting round. Following that, mutual up cards are dealt singly, each followed by a betting round, right to the end. Hence, instead of each player receiving a final down card, the seventh card is another up card, mutual to all hands. Since each player receives only two down cards, this game can accomodate twenty-four players before the pack is exhausted.

Mutual of Omaha

This is exactly like Omaha but with an *insurance* proviso that adds zip to the game. After the seventh card has been dealt, there is a pause before the final betting rounds; and each player, beginning at the dealer's left, has the privilege of *buying* an extra down card for a specified price. That can be half the size of the pot as it stands at the start of the final round; or in a low-limit game, it can be an amount equal to the entire pot. In either case, each player who *insures* his hand must contribute that amount to the pot.

Let's assume a player is holding the **K** and **9 ♦** as down cards, with the **J ♦, 9♠, K♠, 10 ♥, 5 ♦** as the five mutual up cards. All he has is Two Pair (K, K, 9, 9), but he has four chances of picking up a King or a Nine for a Full House. Failing that, he has nine chances for a Flush if he is dealt a Diamond; and four for a Straight if he gets a Queen (K, Q, J, 10, 9). Buying an *insurance* down card would be a wise investment.

Amarillo

Omaha again, but in this case with restrictions. The cards are dealt and bet exactly as in Omaha but in making up his hand, a player *must* use *both* hole cards among the five he chooses. Ordinarily, whenever the five up cards from a *pat* hand, as a Straight, Flush or Full House, all players would disregard their hole cards and simply split the pot, unless one could come up with a higher top card for a Straight or Flush. But in Amarillo there would be no pot splitting, as each player would have to make up whatever he could by adding his two down cards to three of the up cards. Of course, if a Diamond Flush should be showing on the board and he happened to hold two Diamonds in the hole, he would be sitting pretty. But that seldom happens.

Hold 'Em

Also called Hold Me, and Hold Me Darling, this is Omaha in stepped-up form, due to a reduction of the betting rounds. Each player is dealt two down cards and there is an immediate round of betting, beginning at the dealer's left on the strength of those two cards alone. Generally, a player will stay on a Pair, two parts of a Straight Flush, two toward a Flush, or two toward a fairly high Straight, while in a low-limit game, some will chance it with a high card like an Ace or King, regardless of the other card.

Next, three cards are dealt face up in the center of the table. These are known as the *flop* and belong to every player. Thus each player, with his own two cards and the three *mutuals* in the flop, already has the equivalent of a five card Poker hand. A betting round follows and may prove spirited if a high Pair shows in the flop, as a player holding a Pair of his own will figure that he has a good chance for a Full House. Straight and Flush prospects in the flop are also conducive to strong betting.

Next, a fourth up card is dealt, followed by a betting round; and then a fifth up card, followed by a final betting round. Each player who calls forms a five card hand from his own down cards and the mutual up cards, just as in Omaha or its parent game of Seven Card Stud. In all, there are only four betting rounds and the big test comes on the last two, which may make or break a player's prospects for a winning hand.

XII

PUSH POKER

This covers various games of the Stud type in which a player may dispose of unwanted cards by pushing them along to the player at his left. The simplest and most popular form is commonly termed:

Take It or Leave It

This is played like Five Card Stud, but the dealer pauses after dealing the first up card to the player on his left. If the player likes the card, he keeps it; if not, he pushes it to the player on his left and is dealt another card instead. The second player has the privilege of keeping such a card or pushing it along to receive another and this continues around to the dealer. If he receives a card he doesn't want, he simply discards it and deals himself another.

Whenever a player accepts a card, the deal is simply resumed where it left off; and after all players have received an up card, there is a round of betting, as in regular Five Card Stud. That done, the process is repeated after all players have received a second up card, a third, and finally a fourth, with the players turning up their hole cards after the final round. By agreement, each player may be given the option of replacing his hole card at the finish, by discarding it and receiving another down card instead. This can be followed by an extra betting round.

Shove Them Along

Though this term is interchangeable with Take It or Leave It, it also denotes a more liberal version of the game, wherein a player may shove along *any* up card he does not want, instead of the one just dealt to him. With the option of replacing the hole card included, this game becomes liberal indeed.

Pay As You Push

In both games just described, rules are often added whereby a player may be required to pay a specified number of chips for the privilege of (a) pushing an up card other than the one just dealt; (b) exchanging his down card for another; (c) pushing along the up card dealt to him. Any of these rules can be invoked by agreement.

Pass The Trash

Also inelegantly styled Pass the Garbage, this game begins with a deal of seven cards to each player, who holds them as a concealed hand, exactly as in Draw Poker. From this seven, he selects the three that he wants least and lays them face down. When all players are ready, each pushes along his three to the player on his left, who takes them into his hand. Bets are made before the cards are passed and afterward, with each player considering his prospects toward a five card hand.

That done, each player discards two of his cards, reducing his hand from seven to five. Each then selects a card from his hand and these are *rolled* by turning them face up on the table. A round of betting follows; then a second card is rolled, followed by a betting round; then a third, with bets; and a fourth, with bets. At this point, each player still in the game has one card in his hand and four face up. After the bets are equalized, the final cards are shown, as in Five Card Stud, and the best hand takes the pot.

The unusual feature of this game is that a player who has a *pat* five card hand to start, is forced to break it up with his original discard. Example: With **K ♦, J ♦, 8 ♦, 7 ♦, 5 ♦, J ♠, 8 ♣,** he has a Diamond Flush in hand, but must discard the **5 ♦** along with the **J ♠** and **8 ♣**, trusting that he will pick up another Diamond from the player on the right. Or he might decide to discard the **K ♦, 7 ♦** and **5 ♦**, hoping to catch a Jack or an Eight to give him a Full House: J, J, J, 8, 8.

That problem is avoided in a game called:

Screwy Louie

This is Pass the Trash, but with the trash consisting of only two cards instead of three, enabling a player to retain his *pat hand* throughout — provided of course, that he holds one to begin with. In both Pass the Trash and Screwy Louie, the second betting round is often eliminated, reducing the total to five: one preliminary and four rolls. This makes for a faster game. With either game, cards may be shoved to the right instead of the left, if preferred.

XIII

FORMS OF MINI-POKER

This refers to games that follow the general pattern of standard Poker, either Draw or Stud with the first card down and others up, but with *less than five cards* making up a player's hand.

Four Card Poker

Four cards are dealt to each player, as in Draw or Stud with final hands usually ranked in this order: Four of a Kind, Straight Flush, Three of a Kind, Flush, Straight, Two Pair, Pair, Ace-High. Other orders of ranking may be specified by agreement. The game can be played high low and with wild cards, preferably Deuces Wild.

Three Card Poker

Three cards are dealt to each player, with final hands ranking: Straight Flush, Three of a Kind, Flush, Straight, Pair, Ace-High. When played as High Low Stud, it is known as Monte and in some groups, Straights and Flushes are not counted. Other variants are allowable.

Two Card Poker

Two cards to each player, with all going for a Pair, or failing that, High Card. When played high low it is termed Dynamite and with Deuces Wild, Hurricane. Variants have names like Gruesome Twosome, Double Trouble and others.

One Card Poker

One card face down to each player. High card wins; or high low split, as preferred. Familiarly termed Lazy Lucy.

XIV

POVERTY POKER

In many sociable Poker sessions, each player is allowed to buy a specified number of chips, but no more, the purpose being to keep a player's losses within bounds that he can reasonably afford. When a player has used up his quota of chips, which is usually specified in terms of so many stacks, he drops out of the game. That rule works nicely if the stakes are not too high, or the session too prolonged, otherwise the game may be ruined. Nobody wants to sit around just watching other people play Poker; furthermore, the table will be one player short, or perhaps more if others lose all their chips too rapidly.

Poverty Poker solves that problem and therefore should be considered as a special type of game for social play. There are two different methods which may be used, so they will be considered separately.

One is to give the player an additional stack of chips, which are charged against him with the understanding that he must pay off all he can at the conclusion of the game. If he continues to lose and comes out still shorter at the finish, nobody is the loser, because the other players will have won back some of the chips to which the banker staked him and he will simply return the rest. It's not a case of the others sharing the player's losses, although the dealer charges them pro rata for whatever chips the loser would have returned, because by the old rule, the losing player would have dropped from the game before the banker gave him credit.

For example: In a six player game, one player, Andy, loses his original quota of chips and is staked to a stack of 50 more. He loses 25 of those, and turns in the remaining 25. To make up the difference, the other five players contribute five chips each to the bank, before cashing in their own chips. That represents the total of 25 that they won back from Andy.

However, suppose that Andy's luck turned for the better after he was staked to the 50 chips. He would then have paid them back to the banker, squaring his account, and would have continued to play with the chips that he had won. Still, the other players would have no cause to complain that Andy had been winning on *their* money. If they had let him buy those 50 chips instead of getting them on credit, he would have cashed them in, so actually, nobody loses more than he should have.

Even if the player who gained a *free ride* should stage a comeback and go home the big winner, the others should have no gripe. If one of them had lost sufficiently to acquire chips on credit, he would have had that same privilege. So they should regard the whole thing as personal insurance against too great a loss and let it go at that.

Yet there is one flaw in the procedure just described. Suppose that Andy, given his stack of free chips, decides that since he has nothing to lose but a lot to gain, he might as well bet on anything. In Stud Poker, he will *stay* or even *raise* on hands that he would ordinarily turn down. In Draw, he will try to *fill* such dubious holdings as an Inside Straight or a Three Flush. If other players retaliate with the same tactics, they will run the risk of real losses, yet if they accuse Andy of luring them into a losing game, he can honestly insist that he is following the usual tactics employed by many people when trying to recoup their losses.

That can be counteracted by playing Poverty Poker according to its alternate set of rules, which run as follows:

As soon as a player like Andy puts up the last chip of his

original quota, he continues to play without using any chips at all, but he is only allowed to *stay* when other players bet. He cannot bet or raise; but when everyone else has called, he shows his hand along with the rest. He is included in every deal and is allowed to deal in his turn, without putting up an ante. This continues until he comes up with a winning hand. He takes that pot and resumes play as an active player.

By agreement, whenever a player is down to his last few chips, he may be allowed to cash them in and start the next deal on a *poverty* status. Otherwise, he may run out of chips in the middle of a betting round during the next deal. That still does not matter, for he would continue to tag along in that deal without betting any further. If he wins, he resumes play on regular basis during the next deal, so it works out just the same.

XV

DOUBLE DRAW

In a game involving five players or less, Double Draw provides action not found in the standard game. It encourages players to stay on anything — and in some cases nothing — with real hopes of good results. This overcomes a weakness frequently encountered in regular Draw Poker, where players toss in their cards rather than take a long chance on filling a slightly promising hand. In Double Draw, you don't run into hands where the player who opens the pot wins it with no competition, or the deal moves along because nobody opened it at all.

Instead, most players usually stay, because in this game each player is allowed to draw twice, so that the odds against him are often cut in half. Also, the feature of the Double Draw may give him a chance of improving his hand to a point where it may become an excellent *one draw* hand, the kind that he would have preferred in the first place. In short, it isn't just a case of drawing twice in hope of hitting once; a player may change his objective between draws, which makes the game all the more intriguing, as a sample hand will show.

First, however, a description of the game is in order. Briefly, the cards are dealt exactly as in standard Draw Poker, with the usual round of preliminary betting. A player should be allowed to open on anything, in order to encourage participation.

Following the preliminary betting round, active players draw, each being limited to three cards, and another betting round follows. This, however, is not final. The players are still betting on prospect, except for those who are satisfied with what they hold. As soon as all bets have been called, the players draw again, again with a limit of three cards. Another round of betting follows and whoever has the highest hand at the showdown becomes the winner.

Now for the sample hand that will graphically illustrate the possibilities of Double Draw:

Players	Hands				
Dave	J♣	6♣	3♣	9♦	4♥
Dean	J♠	10♥	8♣	4♣	2♦
Dick	A♦	9♣	8♦	7♠	2♠
Doug	A♠	9♥	7♣	6♠	5♥
Duff	K♦	K♠	10♦	3♦	2♣

Dave opens and the rest stay. In a game of regular Draw Poker, only Duff would have good reason to open, with his Pair of Kings. But with Double Draw, all were willing to chance it, and the first *draw* ran as follows:

Dave kept the **J♣**, **6♣** and **3♣**, as three parts to a Flush, discarding the **9♦** and **4♥**. He picked up the **5♦** and **4♠**. No help toward his Flush.

Dean kept the **J♠**, **10♥** and **8♣**, as three parts toward a Straight. He discarded the **4♣** and **2♦**, picking up the **8♠** and **8♥**, a lucky draw indeed.

Dick kept the **9♣**, **8♦** and **7♠**, as three parts toward a Straight that at least was open-ended. He discarded that **A♦** and **2♠**, picking up **J♥** and **2♥**; not as good as he hoped.

Doug kept the **9♥**, **7♣**, **6♠**, **5♥**, four parts toward an inside Straight. He discarded the **A♠** and picked up the **9♠**.

Duff kept his Pair of Kings and discarded the rest: **10♦**, **3♦** and **2♣**. He picked up the **Q♠**, **J♦** and **10♣**. No improvement on his original Pair, but something with new prospects.

Note that in standard Draw, this should have given Duff a win with a Pair of Kings against no opposition; but with everybody staying on practically nothing, Dean would have gained a freak win with his Three Eights. But now, *with another draw to come,* the players are able to rearrange their hands for new appraisals that might bring real results:

Players	Hands				
Dave	6♣	5♦	4♠	3♣	J♣
Dean	8♣	8♠	8♥	J♠	10♥
Dick	J♥	9♣	8♦	7♠	2♥
Doug	9♠	9♥	7♣	6♠	5♥
Duff	K♠	Q♠	J♦	10♣	K♦

Look how things have looked up!

Dave has forgotten the Flush possibilities that didn't improve. He finds himself holding a *bobtail* Straight, with a sequence of 6, 5, 4, 3. So he discards the J♣, hoping to pick up a Seven or a Deuce to complete his Straight, with a one card draw.

Dean, sitting pretty with an unexpected Three Eights, discards the J♠ and 10♥, hoping to improve his Triplets.

Dick still feels that a Straight is his only hope, if he can catch a Ten to fill his J, 9, 8, 7. In a regular game, he would drop rather than try to fill an *inside* Straight, but here, he stays, discarding the 2♥ and drawing one card.

Doug now has a Pair of Nines, so decides to go along with those rather than try again to fill the inside Straight (9, 7, 6, 5) which he has already missed.

Duff finds himself the lucky holder of a King-high *bobtail* Straight, which needs only an Ace or a Nine to make it a potentially big winner. He discards his K♦, drawing one card.

Now, let us see how well each player fared with his *second draw.* Here is how the hands appeared at the finish in this particular case:

Players			Hands			
Dave	6♣	5♦	4♠	3♣	4♦	(Drew 4♦)
Dean	8♣	8♠	8♥	K♣	7♦	(Drew K♣, 7♦)
Dick	J♥	10♠	9♣	8♦	7♠	(Drew 10♠)
Doug	9♠	9♥	A♣	7♥	3♠	(Drew A, 7, 3)
Duff	K♠	Q♠	J♦	10♣	6♦	(Drew 6♦)

Dave failed to make his Straight, which was all for the best, as it would have lost anyway. Dave, as opener, threw in his now worthless hand. Dean promptly bet on the strength of his Three Eights, for though he hadn't improved them, they still could rate tops. Dick, however, had filled his inside Straight by drawing the 10♠, giving him J, 10, 9, 8, 7, so he raised. Doug dropped. Duff, who drew the 6♦, was forced to drop, though if he'd made his Straight, it would have topped Dick's. Dean called with his Three Eights and Dick won with his Jack-high Straight.

An analysis of these hands shows that in Double Draw, you are not looking for bigger hands than in the standard game. You are simply increasing your chances for improvement, so when it comes to the showndown, you can expect more competition than when players are limited to a single draw. That not only puts more punch into the game; it puts more money in the pot, which is what every good Poker player wants. "The better the hands, the bigger the bets" is an old Poker adage that holds true with Double Draw.

Taking the players in order:

Dave began by going for a Flush, hoping that if he drew a single Club to go with the three he already had, he might land another on his second draw. But when he found himself with a 6, 5, 4, 3 sequence, he went after a Straight instead. In short, he was glad to go for *less,* not more than he originally intended.

Dean's lucky draw of Three Eights was the sort that could have occurred in a standard game, as it happened on the first draw; and the second draw, it should be noted, was of no help whatever. He'd wanted a Straight; he settled for Three Eights.

Dick took both draws to build a 9, 8, 7 *bobtail* into a full-fledged Jack-high Straight. That is typical of Double Draw, but he only made what he was after; nothing more.

Doug went after an inside Straight on his first draw; then made a wild stab with a Pair of Nines, hoping for Triplets that he didn't make, so he was on the downgrade rather than the up.

Duff, who turned a Pair of Kings into a promising *bobtail* on his first draw, was the only player who threatened to exceed his original expectation of Three Kings. But he didn't get his Straight on his second draw.

So the hands ran rather true to form, which happens often in Double Draw. Just remember that if you are lucky enough to fill a Straight or Flush with the aid of two draws, somebody else may do the same. So set your sights high enough to start, to insure a payoff at the finish.

Double Draw makes an excellent form of Dealer's Choice and can be played with more than five players by gathering discards after the first draw and shuffling them in with the remainder of the pack, thus replenishing it for the second draw.

XVI

COLOR POKER

This fast-moving version of our *national game* provides keen competition in which most players will stay to the bitter end, just to see what luck will bring. This makes it a popular innovation when playing Dealer's Choice and though luck is a predominant factor, at times there are chances for sharp calculation that will serve a player well. Perhaps the greatest merit of Color Poker is its simplicity, for in its most popular form, it is played precisely like standard Draw Poker, but with this proviso:

In the showdown, hands composed entirely of *one color* — either red or black — take precedence over all others. That is, when such hands appear, all others are eliminated. At first thought, this does not sound too restrictive, considering that there are twenty-six cards of each color in the pack. But closer study will refute this and in actual play, you will find that you may have to break up some very nice hands, such as Three of a Kind or a Straight, in order to conform to the color requirement. Also, and even more important, certain types of hands are impossible with cards of only one color, as you have only two suits available: Diamonds and Hearts with a Red Hand; Clubs and Spades with a Black Hand. This eliminates such potent hands as Four of a Kind, a Full House, or even Three of a Kind.

The following deal will illustrate the various techniques of betting and drawing in a typical game of Color Poker with six players involved:

Al	J♣	J♠	10♠	10♥	5♦
Bob	A♣	K♣	8♠	K♥	7♥
Cal	A♠	Q♠	10♣	5♠	4♥
Doc	K♦	J♥	9♥	6♥	6♦
Ed	9♣	8♣	4♣	2♣	6♠
Fred	Q♦	9♦	8♦	7♠	4♠

The first player, Al, opens and is forced to break a nice Two Pair (J, J, 10, 10) when he discards the **10♥** and **5♦**, to go after an All Black hand. It's well worth a try, since he still has a Pair of Jacks, a potential winner if he draws two black cards.

Bob has to give up a Pair of Kings to conform to the color rule; nevertheless, he stays, discarding the **K♥** and **7♥**, even though it means a two-card draw. After all, his three black cards are topped by A-K, which should win over almost any other High-card hand.

Cal naturally tosses out the **4♥** and calls for just one card, hoping to get a black, which will give him an A-Q High; and possibly something better if he pairs one of his four black cards.

Doc stands pat. He already has an All Red hand with a Pair of Sixes, and since all three players have drawn cards, Doc's hand is tops to date.

Ed furnishes the first dilemma. His hand is All Black, but only Nine High, which would be good enough to stay, if he knew that nobody else already had it made, where Color is concerned. But since Doc stood pat, he is probably holding a one-color hand with something higher than a Nine. So Ed discards his **6♠**, hoping to draw a Club for a Flush; or at worst, a high Spade to keep his hand All Black.

Fred, needing a two-card draw to make his hand All Red, might ordinarily drop, since he knows that Doc already has his color made. But with three Diamonds almost in sequence, a lucky two-card draw could give him a Diamond Flush or a Red Straight, so he stays.

Now, let's see how the draw turned out:

Al: **J♣, J♠, 10♠ — 7♣, 2♦**

This hand is a *bust,* since Al failed to make Black.

Bob **A♣, K♣, 8♠ — 3♠, 3♥**

Also a *bust,* since Bob failed to make Black.

Cal **A♠, Q♠, 10♣, 5♠ — 9♠**

Cal bets, figuring that his All Black hand headed by A,Q,10 may top Doc's *pat hand.*

Doc **K♦, J♥, 9♥, 6♦, 6♥**

With a Pair of Sixes in his All Red hand, Doc sizes Cal for something like an Ace-High, so he raises.

Ed **9♣, 8♣, 4♣, 2♣ — 7♦**

Ed fluffed his one-card draw, getting a red card instead of the Club he wanted, so he drops.

Fred **Q♦, 9♦, 8♦ — Q♥, 5♥**

A draw of two Hearts gives Fred an All Red hand and instead of a Straight or Flush, he catches a Pair of Queens and raises on the strength of them.

Al and Bob drop automatically, while Cal, worried by the two raises, also drops though he has five black cards. Doc calls with his pat hand. Ed has already dropped, so the showdown is between Doc and Fred, who raised Doc. Fred's Pair of Red Queens win over Doc's Pair of Red Sixes.

To keep the game moving fast, it is played with the simple rule that anyone who fails to fill an All Red or All Black hand is immediately ruled out, as described in the sample deal. This means that sometimes a lucky player will pick up a soft pot practically by default, since nobody else can qualify with a *color hand,* but that is all part of the game.

So, too, is the fact that occasionally nobody can stay, so in that case, the pot remains intact. The deal moves on and everybody antes, with a bonus awaiting the player who comes

up with the winning hand, since he will collect the whole pot.
There is, however, a variant called:

Color Poker
With Bluff

Here, the original procedure is the same. Players open, draw and bet exactly as in standard Poker, but anyone failing to fill a color can stay in the game and bluff it out. A player who stands pat and raises to the full limit can thus scare out others who may have four parts to an All Red or All Black but don't want to risk trying to fill it. Of course, the *pat hand* can be a *bust* to start with, just as a player can bluff on anything in regular Draw Poker.

After the draw, if the opener bets and nobody calls him, he naturally takes the pot without showing his hand. But if he is called, or if he checks to start and others do the same, the hands are shown and the highest of one color wins. If nobody has an All Red or All Black hand, the highest hand with four of one color is the winner on the basis of Four Card Poker. If nobody has a hand with four of one color, the pot goes to the hand that has the highest three of one color.

Rank of Hands in Color Poker

Five of One Color	Four of One Color	Three of One Color
Straight Flush	4-Straight Flush	3-Straight Flush
Flush	Four Flush	Three Flush
Straight	Four Straight	Three Straight
Two Pair	Two Pair	One Pair
One Pair	One Pair	High Card
High Card	High Card	—

131

XVII

SIX CARD POKER

Here is a modern form of Poker that adds spice to the grand old game and deserves the increasing popularity that is coming its way. It may be played as a game in its own right, with variants that will be described, or it may be introduced as a form of Dealer's Choice in regular Poker sessions.

Every form of the game is played with Deuces Wild, which is essential toward making up special hands which would otherwise be impossible. To make it still stronger, both Jokers can be included as wild cards, making a 54-card pack. The fact that these cards are *wild* does not make Six Card Poker a *wild game*. Far from it! Though the wild cards play a vital part, they depend upon the others to stabilize the situation, as will be seen.

In Six Card Poker, each player is dealt a hand consisting of six cards, instead of five, from which he hopes to form a Six Card Hand. Those are rated as follows:

Six of a Kind: Highest: A, A, A, A, A, A

Since there are only four Aces in the pack, such a hand must obviously include wild Deuces, so it could run: A, A, A, A, 2, 2; A, A, A, 2, 2, 2; A, A, 2, 2, 2, 2.

With Jokers also wild, there would be more chance of a player holding a Big Six, or Six of a Kind, as such a hand is termed. It is quite as possible to hold Six Kings, Six Queens, and so on down the line.

Six Straight Flush: Highest: **A♥, K♦, Q♥, J♥, 10♥, 9♥**.

Here, Deuces are not needed to complete the required combination, but they are frequently a big help. For example, a hand composed of **Q♣, 2♥, 10♣, 9♣, 2♦, 7♣**, would rate as **Q♣, J♣, 10♣, 9♣, 8♣, 7♣**.

Fours with a Pair: A, A, A, A, 10, 10 represents a *natural* hand of this type; but Deuces can also be involved, as 2, K, K, K, = K, K, K, K with 5, 5; or 2, 2, 9, 9 = 9, 9, 9, 9, with 2, 7 = 7, 7.

Double Triplets: Q, Q, Q with 8, 8, 8. This can only occur as a *natural,* because if either Trip included a Deuce, it could be transferred to the other, to make Fours with a Pair.

Six Flush: **A♥, K♥, J♥, 7♥, 5♥, 3♥** or its equivalent with one or more Deuces, as **2♣, 2♥, J♦, 7♦, 5♦, 3♦**, which would represent **A♦, K♦, J♦, 7♦, 5♦, 3♦**.

Six Straight: J, 10, 9, 8, 7, 6 of mixed suits, or its equivalent of J, 2, 9, 8, 2, 6 = J, 10, 9, 8. 7, 6.

Three Pair: A-A, J-J, 7-7 would be a *natural* combo of this type; but Dueces figure much more frequently (10-10, 6-6, 2-4 = 10-10, 6-6, 4-4; or K-K, 2-9, 2-3 = K-K, 9-9, 3-3; or even 2-A, 2-8, 2-5 = A-A, 8-8, 5-5).

In order to qualify as a *Six Card Hand,* all six cards must be used and the player holding the highest six-card combination wins the pot. If nobody holds a Six Card Hand, each player discards a single card and the hands are rated as in regular five-card Poker, with Deuces Wild and the highest standard wins the pot. For example, a player holds: **2♥, 2♣, A♦, J♦, 10♦, 6♠**.

He has Three Aces, but nothing to go with them. The **6♠** spoils his chance for a Six Card Flush, or a Six Card Straight, and he is unable to form Three Pair with his six cards. However, since nobody else happens to have a Six Card Hand, the player discards his **6♠** and lays down his five cards in the following order: **A♦, 2♥, 2♣, J♦, 10♦**.

This is the equivalent of the A, K, Q, J, 10 of Diamonds, giving the player a Royal Flush, which wins over any rival five-card hand, though it could be tied by another Royal Flush.

Note: With Deuces Wild, the highest hand in standard Poker is Five of a Kind, as Q, Q, Q, Q, 2 = Q, Q, Q, Q, Q. and Five of a Kind outranks a Royal Flush. However, in Six Card Poker, the presence of the necessary Deuce (or Deuces) automatically gives the holder a Six Card Hand, consisting of Fours with a Pair. Example: If the player originally held Q, Q, Q, Q, 2, 5, he would declare his Q, Q, Q, Q as Four Queens and add the Deuce to the Five to form a Pair of Fives. In short, there is no Five of a Kind in Six Card Poker.

Six Card Poker
With Draw

This is a highly volatile game, with five players, each receiving six cards in the initial deal (5 X 6 = 30) with enough cards in reserve for each player to draw as many as four (5 X 4 = 20). In fact, the draw can be limited to four cards, as a player is sure to hold at least a Pair or two good cards of the same suit or in sequence. On that basis, the game can include six players, particularly if the Jokers are added as wild cards. A deal of 6 X 6 = 36, with average draws of three cards each come to 3 X 6 = 18. Add those figures, 36 + 18 = 54 and you will have the exact number of cards in the pack. If the deal should go over, you can always fall back on the rule of shuffling the discards in order that the final players can complete their draw.

To show that the game is variable as well as volatile, it will be detailed in the forms just given: Five players, with the 52-card pack, Deuces Wild; then later, six players with the 54-card pack, Deuces and Jokers Wild.

Five players are dealt six-card hands as follows:

Bart	4♣	4♦	Q♥	J♠	9♥	3♥
Bert	K♥	J♣	9♣	8♣	8♦	3♦
Biff	K♦	7♦	7♠	5♠	4♠	3♠
Bill	K♣	Q♣	J♦	9♠	8♠	3♣
Buck	A♦	Q♦	5♦	J♥	7♣	6♠

Bart opens on an *anything* basis and all the others stay, which is fairly customery in Six Card Poker, except when a player has a highly authoritative hand, which nobody has in this case. Each proceeds to draw as follows:

Bart keeps his Pair of Fours and chucks the rest. A Pair at least is something to work from; and Bart doesn't consider three parts to an *inside* Straight (Q, J, 9) as worth much; and the same applies to his three Hearts toward a Flush.

Bert takes a more optimistic view of his hand. With K, J, 9, 8 as four parts toward a King-high Straight, all he needs to draw is one little Deuce, plus a Queen or a Ten, and he will have a Six Straight. So he discards the 8♦ and 3♦.

Biff is even better off. His 7, 5, 4, 3 in Spades has the makings of a Six Card Straight Flush, with either a Six Card Flush or a Six Card Straight as a lesser prospect. Biff discards the K♦ and 7♦. Like Bert, Biff is hoping for a Deuce and something else.

Bill is most optimistic of all. His K, Q, J, 9, 8 needs only a Ten or a Deuce for a Six Card Straight. He discards the 3♣.

Buck has a real mixed up hand, so about the best he can do is hold three Diamonds toward a Flush (A, Q, 5) and discard the odd J♥, 7♣, 6♠.

The draw followed, with varying luck on the part of each player and here is how the hands turned out:

Bart 4♣, 4♦, 10♣, 10♥, 2♣, 6♥
Made *Three Pair by drawing* 10♣, 10♥, 2♣, 6♥.

Bert K♥, J♣, 9♣, 8♣, 6♣, 5♥
No improvement with draw of 6♣ and 5♥.

Biff 7♠, 5♠, 4♠, 3♠, A♣, 4♥

No improvement with draw of A♣ and 4♥.

    Bill   K♣, Q♣, J♦, 10♦, 9♠, 8♠

Made *Six Card Straight* by one-card draw of 10♦.

    Buck   A♦, Q♦, 5♦, 2♠, Q♠, 10♠

Made *Three Queens* (2, Q, Q) by draw of 2♠, Q♠, 10♠.

Bill was the winner with the highest Six Card Hand, a K, Q, J, 10, 9, 8 Six Card Straight. Bart was only a notch below with his Three Pair, 10-10, 6-6, 4-4. None of the others managed to fill a Six Card Hand.

Bart was lucky to make Three Pair, with only a Pair of Fours to start, but that is the type of *break* that Six Card Poker offers. Bart would have won if Bill hadn't made his Six Card Straight, but perhaps Bill deserved to win for getting what he went after. Note that if Buck, who started with a *nothing* hand, had drawn the 5♣ instead of the 10♠, he would have come up with 2-A, Q-Q, 5-5 for Three Pair. So even a seemingly sure loser can come close to being a winner.

Now for the sample game with six players, using a 54-card pack.

Ray:	A♠	Q♦	J♥	10♣	8♣	4♥
Red:	2♦	K♠	K♦	J♠	7♠	4♦
Rip:	Q♥	9♥	8♥	6♣	4♣	3♣
Rod:	2♥	A♣	Q♣	J♣	10♦	5♣
Ron:	A♦	K♣	7♣	6♦	6♠	6♥
Roy:	K♥	Q♠	10♥	9♦	8♠	5♠

Ray opens and decides to go after a Six Card Straight. If he discards the 8♣ and 4♥, his hand will stand A, *, Q, J, 10, *, so he will have to draw both a King and a Nine, though there are six wild cards that will serve as either a King or a Nine. However, if he discards the A♠ and 4♥, he will have Q, J, 10, *, 8 which is an *open-ender*. A King and a Nine will still do; but so will a Nine and a Seven, giving him that much more chance. So he discards the A♠ and 4♥.

Red holds 2♦, K♠, K♦, the equivalent of Three Kings, which offers good prospects for improvement. He discards

J♠, 7♠, 4♦.

Rip has a peculiarly divided hand with two groups of cards forming three parts toward a Straight Flush: Q, 9, 8 in Hearts; and 6, 4, 3 in Clubs. He keeps the Hearts because they are higher and discards the three low Clubs.

Rod already has a standard five card Straight (A, 2, Q, J, 10 = A, K, Q, J, 10). So he is tempted to discard the low **5♣** in hope of drawing a Nine or a Wild Card. But since his **2♥** can be rated as a Club, he has a five card Flush, which is higher than a Straight and he has a much better chance of getting a sixth card for a Flush than this particular Straight. So he keeps the **5♣** and ditches the **10♦**.

Ron decides to keep his Three Sixes, as two Wild Cards or a Wild Card and any Pair would put him in a high bracket. So he discards the **A♦**, **K♣** and **7♣**.

Roy is nicely fixed with five cards toward a potential Six Card Straight. But it is an *inside* Straight, demanding a Jack, Deuce or Joker for a fill. Roy decides to try by discarding the **5♠**.

Here is how it all turned out:

 Ray: **Q♦, J♥, 10♣, 9♠, 8♣, 8♦**

No improvement. Ray drew the Nine (**9♠**) that he wanted, but got the **8♦** instead of a Seven which he also needed.

 Red: **K♠, K♦, 2♦, 7♥, 2♠, 3♠**

Made *Three Pair* by drawing **7♥**, **2♠** and **3♠**, which fell neatly into the order shown: K-K, 2-7 = 7-7; 2-3 = 3-3.

 Rip: **A♥, Q♥, 9♥, 8♥, 3♥, J♦**

Made a five-card Flush by drawing **A♥**, **3♥** and **J♦**. Needed a sixth Heart to qualify.

 Rod: **A♣, 2♥, Q♣, J♣, 9♣, 5♣**

Filled *Six Card Flush* by one-card draw of **9♣**.

 Ron: **6♦, 6♠, 6♥, Joker, 5♥, 3♦**

Stuck with Four Sixes. Draw of Joker, **5♥**, and **3♦** was no help, even with the Wild Card.

 Roy: **K♥, Q♠, Joker, 10♥, 9♦, 8♠**

Filled *Six Card Straight* by draw of Joker for K, Q, J, 10, 9, 8.

Rod won with a high Six Card Flush: A, K, Q, J, 9, in Clubs. Rod had the best prospects going in and came out accordingly. Oddly, if he had gone for his Six Card Straight by keeping the **10♦** instead of the **5♣**, he would have made it with his draw **9♣** giving him an A, K, Q, J, 10, 9, which still would have beaten the second man. Roy, with his K, Q, J, 10, 9, 8. Red, who also made a Six Card Hand, ran third with his Three Pair.

As a further analysis, if Rod, Roy and Red had failed to fill their hands, thus reducing the final play to a standard five card basis, Rod would still have won on the strength of his original five card Flush: A, K, Q, J, 5 in Clubs (with the **2♥** standing for the **K♣**). Even though Rip came through with a five card Ace-high Flush in Hearts, and was hoping he would have a chance to show it, Rod still would have won with his A, K, Q, J, 5 over Rip's A, Q, 9, 8, 3.

Stud Version of
Six Card Poker

Six Card Poker is an excellent game when played as Eight Card Stud with two Jokers and all four Deuces Wild. The 54-card pack accommodates six players, or even a seventh, as one or two are apt to fold their hands early. Each player is dealt two down cards and one up card to start the first betting round. Four more up cards follow, each with a betting round; then each receives a down card for a final betting round.

Play conforms to the rules of Eight Card Stud with wild cards as specified, but when the live players finally turn up their cards, any complete six card hands take precedence over the rest. All such hands are ranked as already described in Six

Card Poker, so the highest *sixer* wins the pot. The simplest way to do this is for each player to turn down the two cards he does not need or want. The final hands can then be compared on a six card basis.

If there are no complete six card hands, each player turns down another card, reducing his hand to five. These hands are rated as in regular Five Card Poker, from Five of a Kind to a mere Pair or less.

Rather surprisingly, if most of the players stay, as they are apt to do in this game, somebody usually comes up with a complete six card hand and often there is close rivalry between two such hands. Note, however, that a complete seven or eight card hand rates only according to its six best cards. Thus, a player holding J, 2, 10, 9, 2, 7, 6, 5 would turn down the 6 and 5, calling his hand a Six Card Straight, Queen High.

XVIII

SEVEN CARD POKER

As an elaboration or follow-up of the Six Card game, Seven Card Poker may sound a trifle fantastic or unmanageable, but such is not the case. Its simplest and most direct form is a six-player game utilizing a 54-card pack with four Deuces and two Jokers as wild cards. Each player contributes a fixed amount to the pot and is dealt nine cards face down, so that the entire pack is dealt.

Each player selects his seven best cards from his hand of nine and the player at the dealer's left checks or bets, as he chooses, while the rest may call, raise, or drop. When those remaining in the game have equalized their bets, they show their hands, which are rated as follows:

Seven of a Kind: Highest A, A, A, A, A, A, A

With six wild cards in the pack, this can run the gamut from Ace, Joker, Joker, 2, 2, 2, 2 to A, A, A, A, Joker, 2, 2 with other combinations in between. It is possible for two players to hold Seven of a Kind, as Q, Q, Q, Q, 2, 2, 2 versus 10, 10, 10, 10, Joker, Joker, 2.

Seven Straight Flush: Highest A♠, K♠, Q♠, J♠, 10, ♠, 9♠, 8♠. Substitute a Deuce or a Joker for any of the cards listed and the hand will be the same.

Five of a Kind With a Pair: K, K, K, K, 2, 7, 7

At least one Wild Card is needed for the Fives and sometimes it takes another to make up the Pair, as J, J, J, 2, 2; K, 2.

Note that this could be called Six of a Kind — J, J, J, 2, 2, 2, but in that case, the hand could not be rated as a complete Seven Card combination.

Fours and Threes: 9, 9, 9, 9, 3, 3, 3

This can be a natural combination, as shown above; or a Wild Card can be included, as: K, K, K, 2; 8, 8, 8.

Seven Flush: A♦, J♦, 9♦, 8♦, 6♦, 4♦, 3♦

Any seven cards of one suit, with Wild Cards allowable as replacements.

Seven Straight: 10, 9, 8, 7, 6, 5, 4 of mixed suits.

These rank as Ace-high, King-high, etc., according to the top card of the sequence, which is Ten-high in the example. Wild Cards can be used as replacements.

Three of a Kind With Two Pair: K-K-K, 10-10, 6-6

Wild Cards can figure in this combination, particularly when a hand lacks a Triplet or is short on Pairs. Typical examples: A-A-Joker, 10-10, 6-6 or 7-7-7, A-2, 8-2.

Seven Card Showdown

In the game as just described, a player must hold a complete hand of seven cards forming one of the listed combinations. Without such a hand, he simply drops out, losing the fixed amount that he contributed at the start. Those who remain bet on the merits of their respective hands, until finally all are shown and the best combo wins. All hands must be shown, to prove that they were valid seven card combinations, as otherwise they should have been dropped.

If nobody holds a seven carder, everybody drops as a matter of course, so the pot remains intact, as a bonus toward the next deal. Usually, someone comes up with a winning hand, because all the Wild Cards have been dealt in the six-handed game.

With less than six players, the action can be spurred by dealing ten cards to each player in a five-player game; and as many as twelve in a four-handed or three-handed game. Otherwise, too many Wild Cards might be left stranded in the pack, causing Seven Card Hands to be too feeble or nonexistant.

Seven Card Poker
With Draw

With five players or less, Seven Card Draw can be played exactly like the Six Card game, except that Seven Card hands are much harder to complete. Hence, this game should be played by the rule that following the draw, the dealer calls upon all players holding complete Seven Card hands to announce the fact, so that they alone can participate in the betting that follows.

If nobody has a Seven Card hand, the dealer calls for Six Card hands; and bets follow on that basis. If nobody has a Six Card hand, which can happen, bets are made according to standard Poker, with five cards to each hand.

Stud Version of
Seven Card Poker

Played as Nine Card Stud, with a 54-card pack, Seven Card Poker can accommodate six players, with all staying to the finish, as they occasionally do. Two Jokers and four Deuces serve as wild cards. Each player is dealt two down cards and one up card before the first betting round. From then on, four more up cards are dealt, each followed by a round of betting. Then come two down cards, each with a betting round.

At the finish, each player still in the game turns up his hole cards and selects seven cards to make a complete hand according to the ranking in Seven Card Poker, provided, of course, that he has the cards with which to do it. The highest such hand wins the pot, and if each player turns down his two discards, the hands can easily be compared and judged.

If there are no complete seven card hands, each player turns down another card in order to form a complete six card hand and any such are rated as in Six Card Poker. Note that these must be complete hands in order to count. If there are no complete six card hands, each player turns down another card, so that the hands can be rated as in regular Five Card Poker, with wild cards as specified. These hands do not have to be complete.

Note that extra cards are not considered when forming or judging a seven card hand. If one player holds an Ace-high Flush of seven Spades, it beats a King-high Flush in Hearts, even if the player with the Heart Flush can show eight or even nine cards of that suit.